NEWPORT Cwmbran, Pontypool & Chepstow

Abersychan	3	Marshfield	30
Bassaleg	17	New Inn	5
Bettws	12	Parc-Seymour	24
Bishpool	16	Penhow	25
Blaenavon	1	Penperlleni	5
Caerleon	15	Ponthir	15
Caerwent	26	Pontnewynydd	4
Caldicot	28	Pontypool	4
Castleton	30	Portskewett	29
Celtic Lakes	18	Redwick	27
Chepstow	31	Ringland	23
City Centre	33	Rogerstone	12
Croesyceiliog	9	Rogiet	28
Cwmbran	7	Shirenewton	26
Duffryn	20	Snatchwood	3
Gaer	19	Somerton	21
Griffithstown	6	St. Arvans	31
Liswerry	21	St. Woolos	19
Llangybi	24	Stelvio	19
Llanover	1	Stow Park	19
Llantarnam	10	Sudbrook	29
Llantrisant	25	Talywain	2
Llanyrafon	10	Underwood	23
Magor	27	Undy	27
Maindee	16	Usk	30
Malpas	13	Wainfelin	4

Streetezee®

NEWPORT
Cwmbran, Pontypool & Chepstow

Key to street plans
Allwedd i blaniau stryd

Street plans drawn at a scale of 4 inches to 1 mile
Aruluniwyd y planiau yn ôl y raddfa 4 modfedd i 1 filltir

Symbol	English	Welsh
M4	Motorway	Traffordd
A48	A road (Trunk road)	Ffordd A (Priffordd)
B4281	B road	Ffordd B
	Through road	Ffordd drwodd
	Dual carriageway	Ffordd ddeuol
	Track/Footpath	Llwybr/Llwybr troed
	Railway	Rheilffordd
	Built up area	Ardal adeiledig
	Recreation ground	Maes chwarae
	Woods and forest	Coedtir a choedwig
	Health centre	Canolfan iechyd
H	Hospital	Ysbytty
	Petrol station	Gorsaf betrol
	Places of worship	Mannau addoliad
	Police station	Gorsaf heddlu
	Post Office	Swyddfa'r Post
	Telephone	Ffon
	Toilet facility	Cyfleustra toiled
P	Car parks (major)	(prif) Maes parcio
	Caravan/camp site	Safloedd carafannau gwersyll
i	Information centre	Canolfan hysbysrwydd
	Golf Course	Maes golff
M	Museum/Theatre	Amgueddfa/Theatr
	Public house	Tafarndy
	House numbers	Rhifau Tai

Blaenavon
(World Heritage Site)
Middle Coedcae
Forge Side
Talywain
Snatchwood
Pentre-Poid
Wainfelin
Varteg
Garndiffaith
Abersychan
Trevethin
Pontnewynydd
Pontypool
Pontymoel

Llanover
Penperlleni
Little Mill
Usk

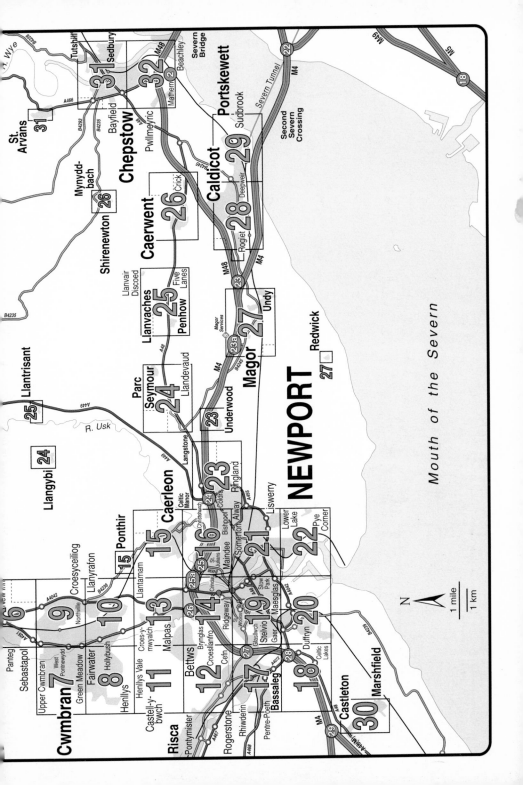

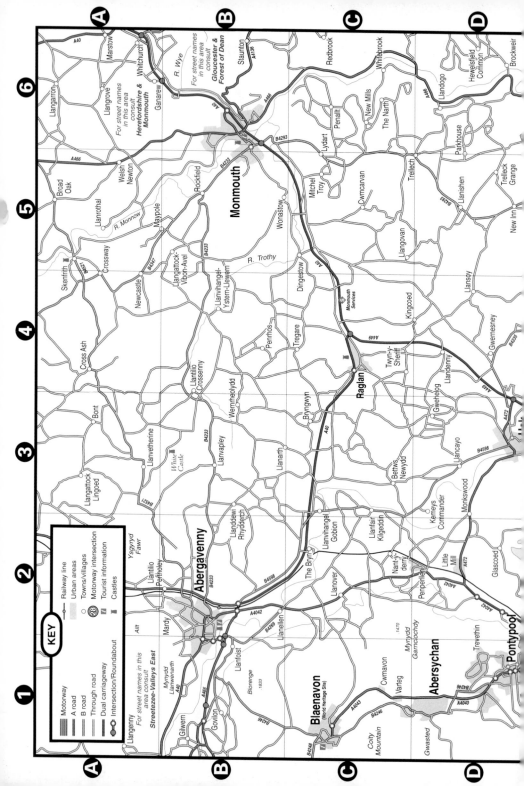

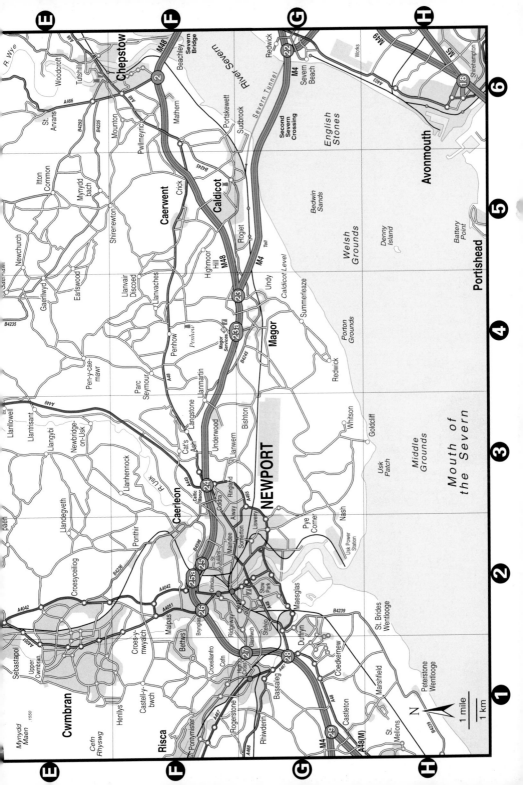

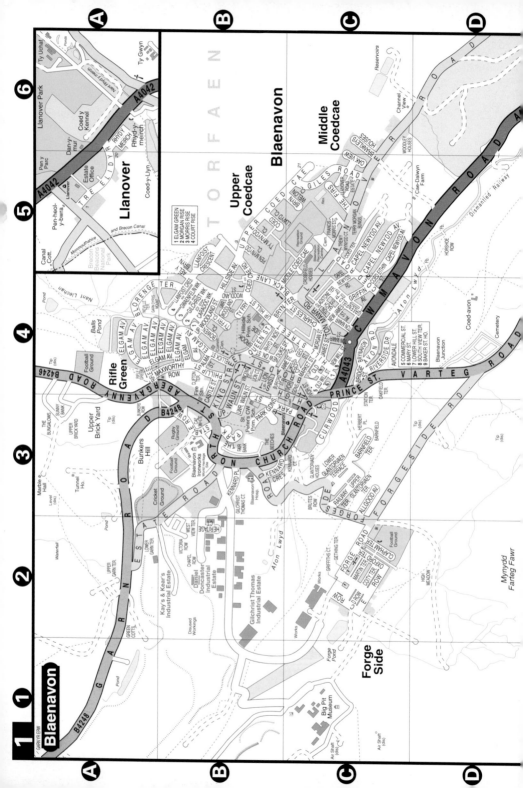

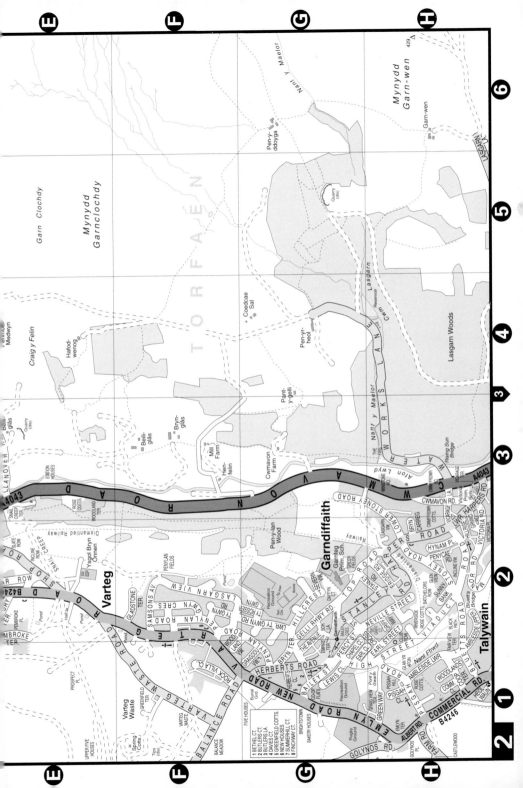

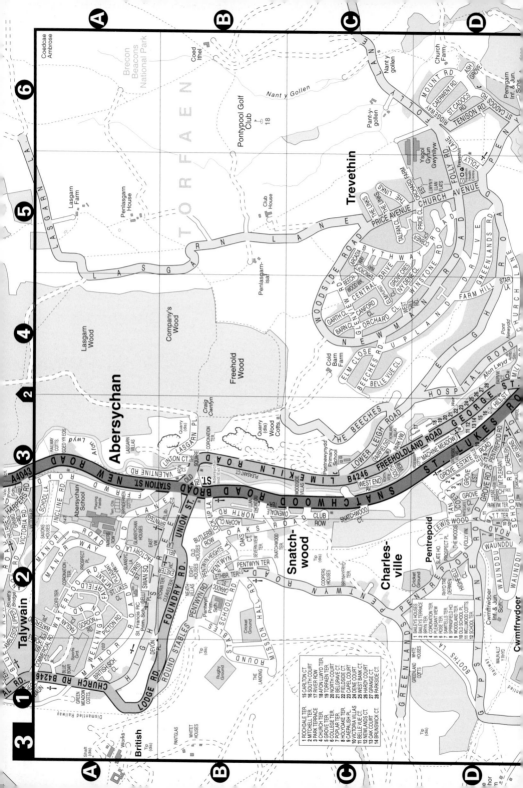

8

A 6
Coedcae Ambrose
Brecon Beacons National Park
Coed Ithel
TORFAEN

B 6
Nant y Gollen
Pontypool Golf Club
18

C 6
Nant y gollen
Church Farm
Church Rd
MOUNT RD
CAERMEN RD
RIDGEWAY
ST CADOCS RD
TENISON RD

D 6
ASH GROVE
Penygarn Inf. & Jun. Schs
ST CADOCS RD
PEN

A 5
Lasgarn Farm
Penlasgarn House
LASGARN LA

B 5
Club House
Penlasgarn-isaf
GARN LANE

C 5
Trevethin
FOLLY LANE
Yspol Gylun Gwyllyw
Trevethin
FOLLY
LLWYN LLAN ELAIS
THE LINKS
PRICE AVENUE
ORCHARD FARM
PRICE CL
THE LINKS
TALFAN RD
CHURCH AVENUE
GREENLANDS RD

D 5
PEN
FOLLY RD
CHURCH RD
Trevethin Health Centre
CHURCH LANE

A 4
Lasgarn Wood

B 4
Company's Wood
Freehold Wood
Penlasgarn-isaf

C 4
WOODSIDE ROAD
BEECH RD
ARCADIA
WOOD VW
CENTRAL
GARTH CLO
CANFORD CL
BARN CLO
ORCHARD
NEW RD
GLENVIEW
GLYNDWR
GROVE CRES
VLY DEN CL
WEST AV
WEST RD
WINSTONE ROAD
FARM HILL DRIVE
STAR LA

D 4
UPLANDS
GREENLANDS RD
CHURCH LANE

3 A 3 / British
Abersychan
A4043 NEW ROAD
Shaft (dis)
Works
Tip (dis)
PANTGLAS
WHITE HOUSES
Dismantled Railway
RAILWAY COTTS
LASGARN VILLAS
LINTON CT
Quarry (dis)
LASGARN PL
THE SQUARE
CORPORATION TER
VALENTINE RD
STATION ST
BROAD ST

B 3
Quarry (dis)
Wood Cotts.
CRAIG CWMFFRWD
LIME KILN ROAD
LOWER LEIGH ROAD
Pentrewynydd Primary School
WEST END AV
PLEASANT CT
FAIRFIELD
SNATCHWOOD ROAD
NORTH RD
ACORN CL
OAKS CT

C 3
THE BEECHES
Cold Barn Farm
ELM CLOSE
BEECHES RD
BELLE VUE CL
HOSPITAL ROAD
LEIGH RD
FREEHOLDLAND ROAD
GEORGE ST
ST LUKES RD
GROVE ESTATE RD
PARK VW
GROVE RD
PENTREPIOD RD
B4246
MACHINE MEADOW
Aton Llwyd
HILST CT
Pont Newydd
MILL RD

D 3 / D 2
CAERLLYN
PENTREPIOD RD
BEECH TER
PARK VIEW TER
SCHOOL

A 2
Talywain
BLUE BARR
BLUETS Bridge
BAT RD
BLAENAVON RD (UPR)
VICTORIA RD
HARPERS RD
SCHOOL LA
INCLINE RD
MANOR ROAD
MANOR WAY
PROSPECT PL
GRANDVIC
MITRE PL
LEWIS
HORSE PONDS
FACTORY LA
EAST VW
BELL LA
UNION ST
FOUNDRY RD
EXETER PL

B 2
Aberschan School
GLANSYCHAN HOUSES
PENTWYN HEIGHTS
PENTWYN RD
RIGHT
LETHBR. TER
PENTWYN TER
PENTWYN TER
SNATCHWOOD TER
SEVERN VIEW
OLD HOUSES
BUTLERS ROW
LOCK UP LA
CLUB ROW
SNATCHWOOD CT
OWENDALE TER

C 2
Snatch-wood
COOPERS HOUSES
BRYNHYFRYD TER
PENTWYN ROAD
GREENLANDS PENTRE

D 2
Pentrepoid
LEWIS WOOD
SLATE HO
THE WOODS
RHYTRE
DEWRAS
FOLLY VW
HIGHFIELD
SPRINGFIELD HO
SAMFIELD
PLEASANT VIEW
CORONATION TER
TAN
GROVE RD
WAUNDDU
WAUNDDU

A 1
BLUE AMBLESIDE RD
COMMERCIAL RD
WATERLOO
RAGLAN
GORDON
PICTON RD
HIGH ST
WELLINGTON ROAD
LODGE RD
ROUND STABLES
DEVON
BRITISH RD B4246
CHURCH RD
GREEN MEADOW COTTS
Sports Gd

B 1
FAIRFIELD
FORMATION
PROSPECT RD
ST FRANCIS RD
ST LUKES RD
GARDEN
MITFIELD
BELLI LA
SWAN SQ
SYCAMORE RD
HEATH PL
Pentwyn Sch
SCHOOL RD
Tip (dis)
Rugby Ground
Cricket Ground

C 1
MISSION HALL RD
ROUND STABLES
The Landing
Tip (dis)

D 1
Cwmffrwdoer
Cwmffrwdoer Inf. & Jun. Sch
GYPSY LANE
GREENLANDS PENTRE
BOOTHS LA
WALNUT YARD
Tip (dis)
RAILWAY
Cricket Ground

Charles-ville

Index (bottom of C1)
1 ROCHDALE TER
2 MITCHELL TER
3 PARK TER
4 CHURCH TER
5 GROVE TER
6 COLLEGE TER
7 POPLAR TER
8 BROOME TER
9 CAERLLISH PL
10 VICTORIA VILLAS
11 BELLE VUE CT
12 NEWLANDS CT
13 OAK CT
14 BRUNSWICK CT
15 CARLTON CT
16 SOUTH COURT
17 RIVER ROW
18 AFON LLWYD TER
19 TORFAEN TER
20 NORTH COURT
21 BELGRAVE CT
22 ELMSIDE CT
23 CHAPEL COURT
24 DENE COURT
25 WEST BANK CT.
26 HARDY COURT
27 GRANGE CT
28 PARKSIDE CT

Index (bottom of D1)
1 BAILEYS HOUSES
2 BAILEYS TERRACE
3 BRYN TER
4 CORONATION TER
5 ELEASANT VIEW
6 SAMFIELD TER
7 SPRINGFIELD HO
8 NOTTAGE CT
9 OLD SCHOOL PL
10 WELLWOOD COTTS
11 WELLWOOD COTTS

A — B — C — D (grid letters top and bottom)
6 5 4 2 3 1 (grid numbers)

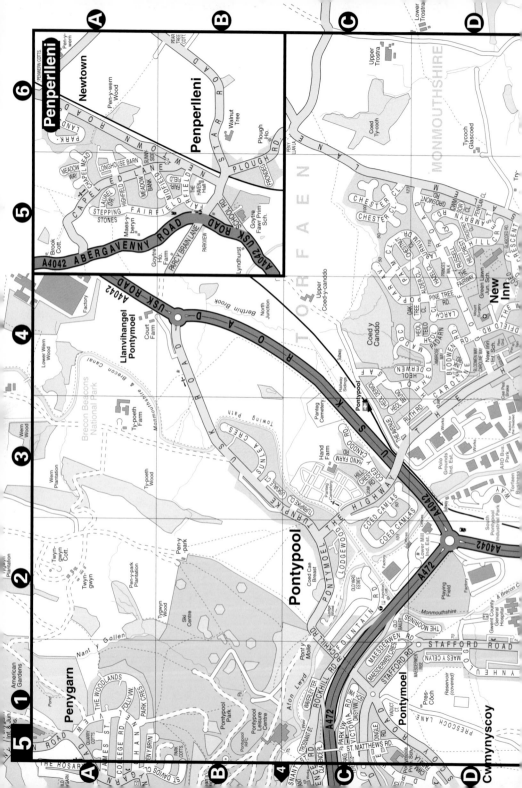

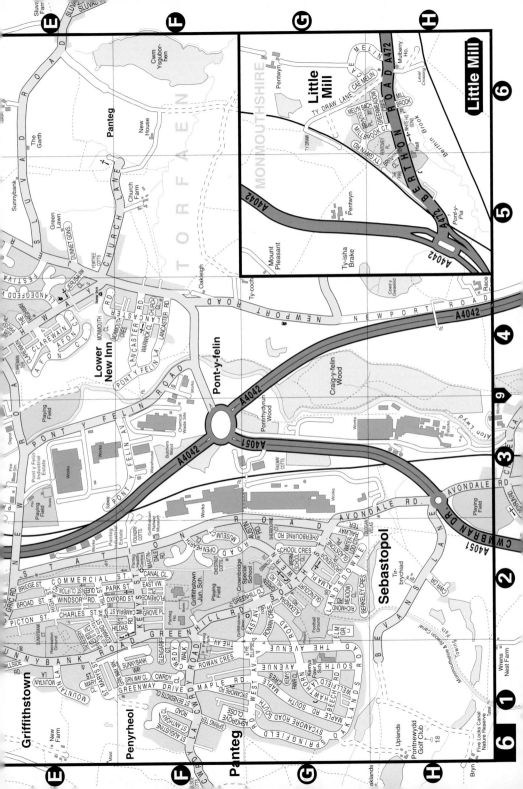

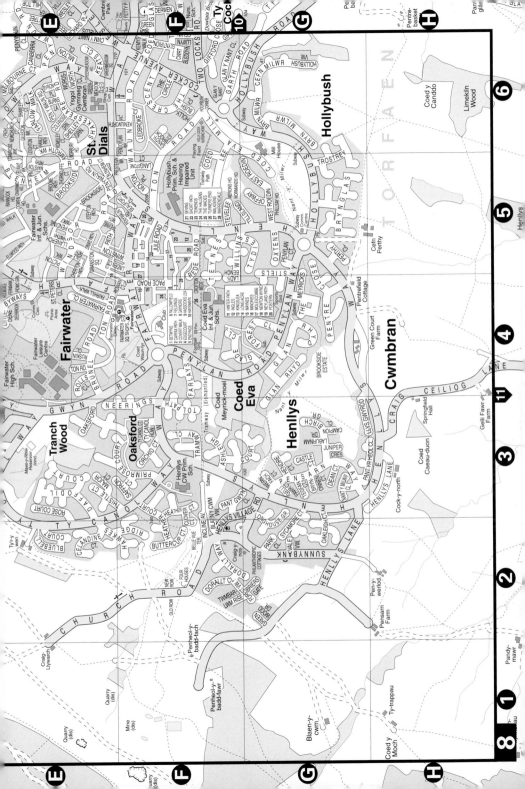

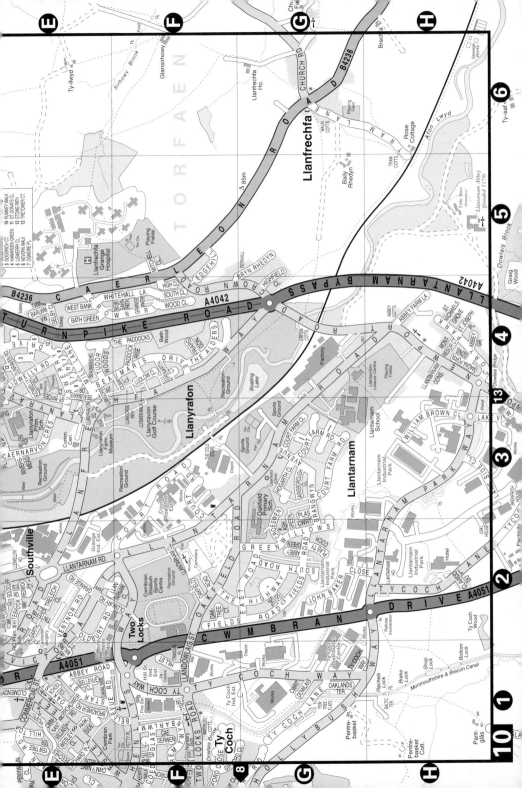

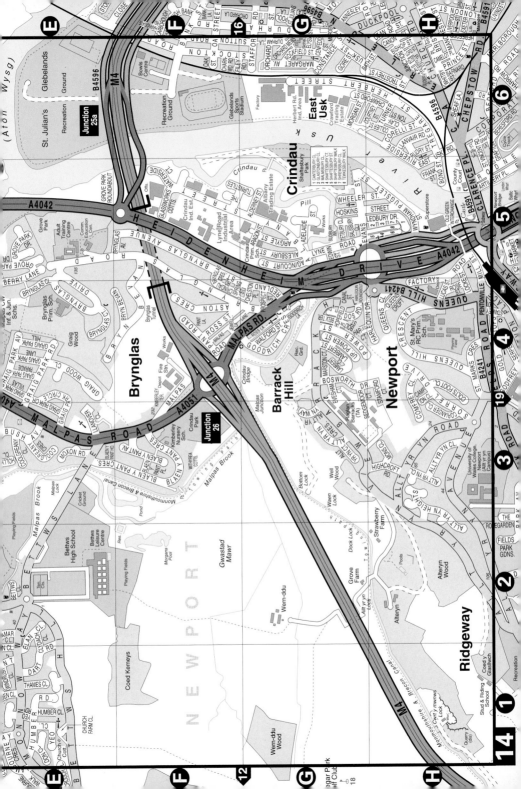

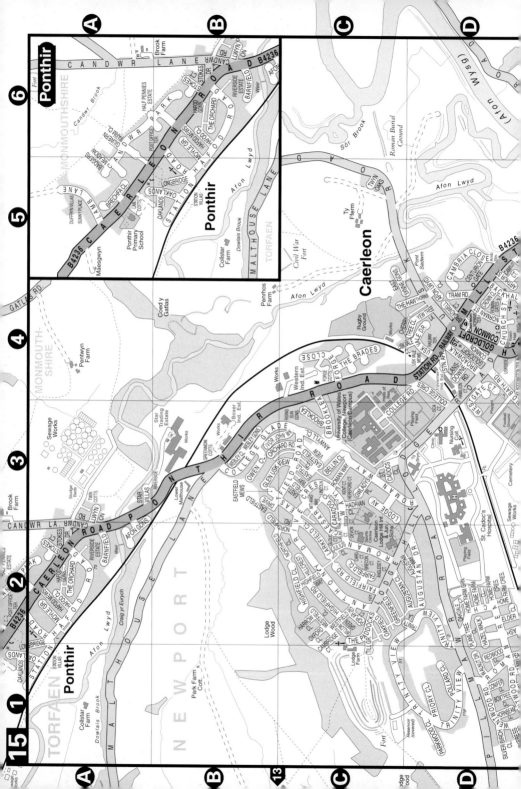

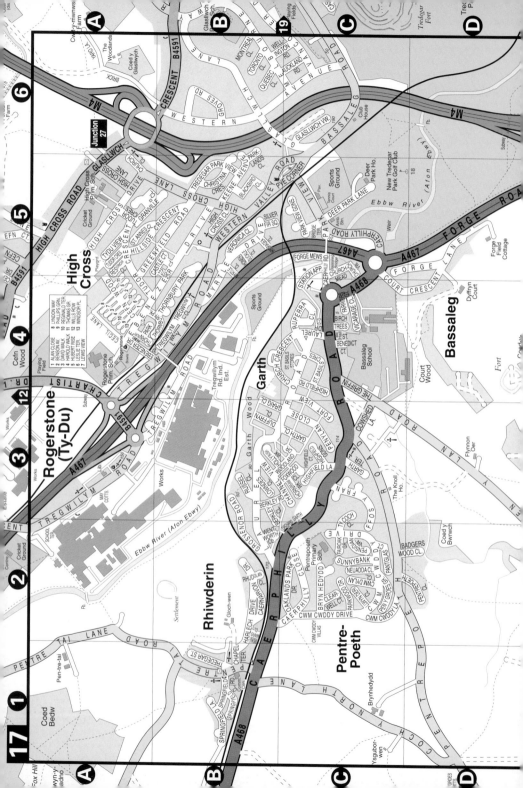

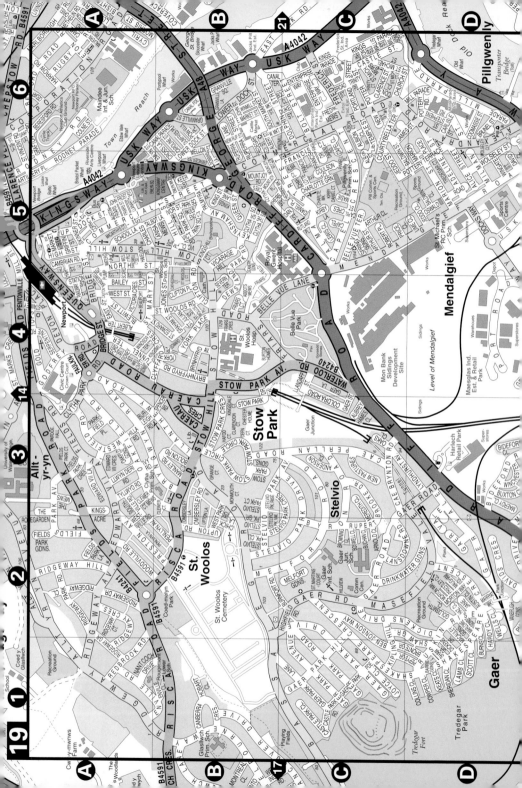

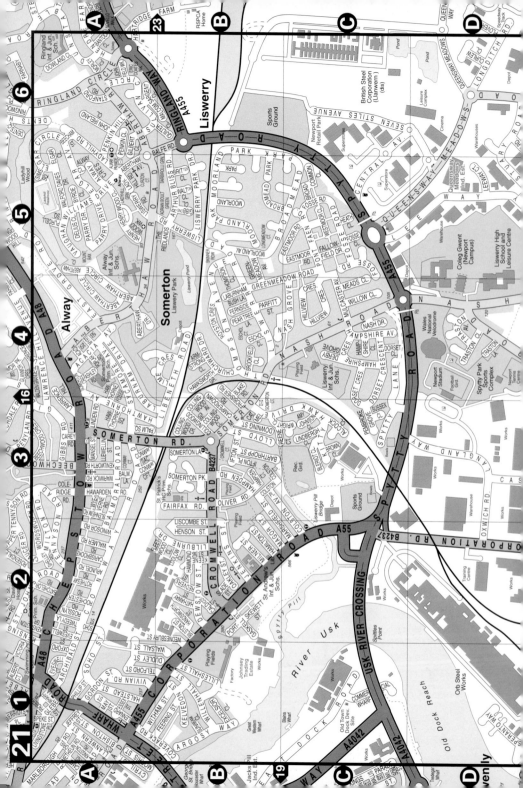

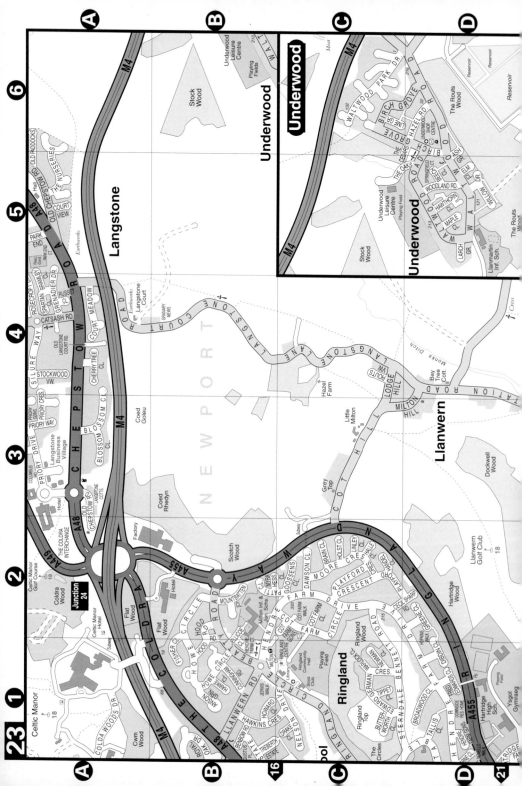

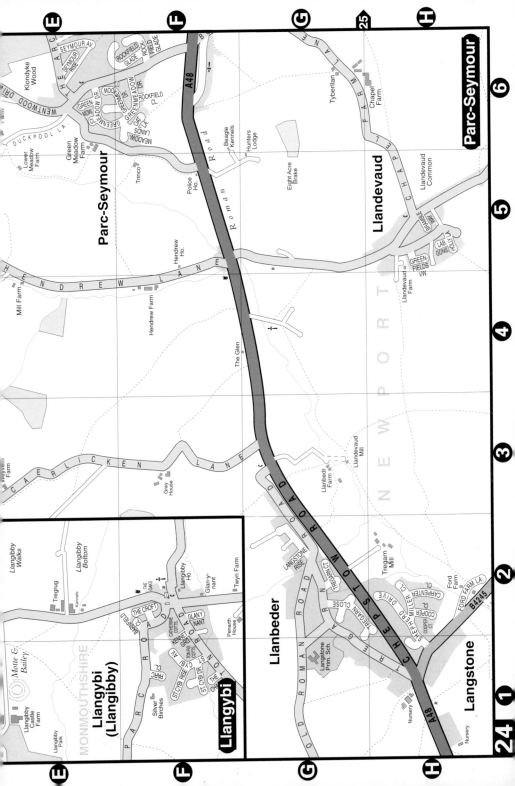

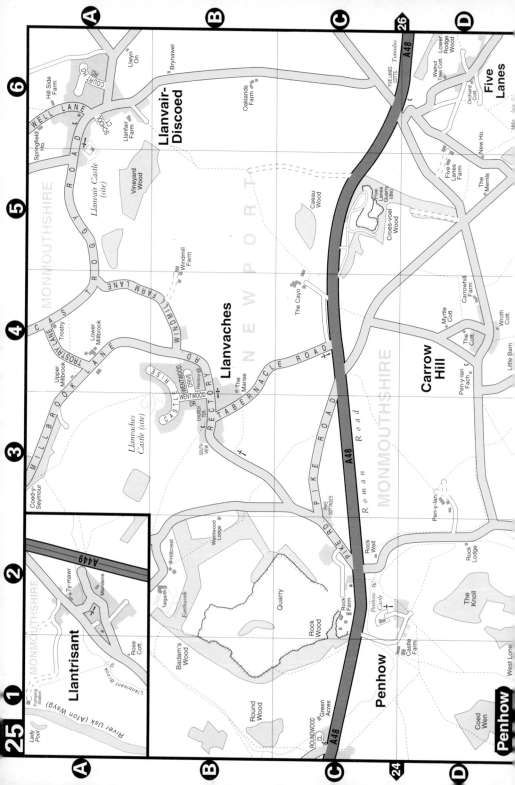

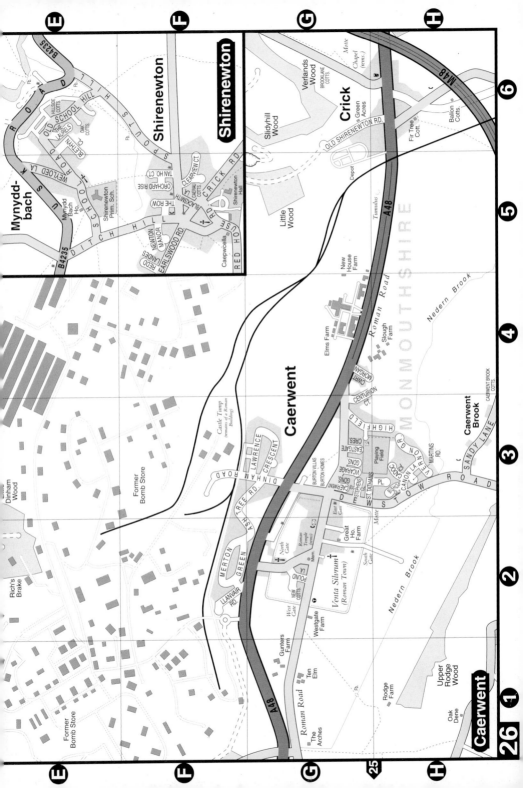

Shirenewton

Shirenewton

Mynydd-bach

Crick

Caerwent

Caerwent Brook

MONMOUTHSHIRE

B4235

WET LOED LAKE

OLD ROAD

SCHOOL HILL

SPOUTS HILL

HILLSIDE COTTS
THE LAURELS
OAK COTTS
BELTHIN CT

MYNYDD BACH HO.

Mynydd Bach Prim. Sch.

REDD LANDES

DITCH HILL

EARL SWOOD RD.

NEWTON MANOR

THE ROW

BLACKSMITH'S

ORCHARD RISE
TAN HO. CT.
CLEARVIEW CT.
CAERAU COTTS
CRICK RD.

Shirenewton Prim. Sch.

Shirenewton Hall

Caepwcella

REDD HOUSE RD.

Slidyhill Wood

Verlands Wood

BROOKLANE COTTS.

Motte

Chapel (rems.)

Green Acres

M48

OLD SHIRENEWTON RD.

Fir Tree Cott.

Ballon Cotts.

Depot

Little Wood

A48

Tumulus

Roman Road

New House Farm

Elms Farm

Slough Farm

CWTI MORGAN

CENTURION CT.

HIGHFIELD

EASTGATE

VICARAGE GDNS

CAERWENT GDNS

BURTON VILLAS
BURTON HOMES

ESTEPS

ST TATHANS

CRES

CROSS

VERNON

CANON LANE

MARTINS RD.

PL.

Playing Field

BISHOPS

Nedern Brook

Caerwent Brook

CAERWENT BROOK COTTS.

SANDY LANE

STOW ROAD

Castle Tump
(remains of a Roman Building)

LAWRENCE CRESCENT

DINHAM ROAD

ASH TREE RD.

MERTON GREEN

LLANVAIR RD.

North Gate

Roman Temple (rems.)

Mem.

POUND
NEW COTTS

Venta Silurum
(Roman Town)

West Gate

Westgate Farm

South Gate

East Gate

Great Ho. Farm

Motte

Nedern Brook

Rich's Brake

Dinham Wood

Former Bomb Store

Gunters Farm

Ten Elm

Rodge Farm

Upper Rodge Wood

Oak Dene

Former Bomb Store

A48

Roman Road

The Arches

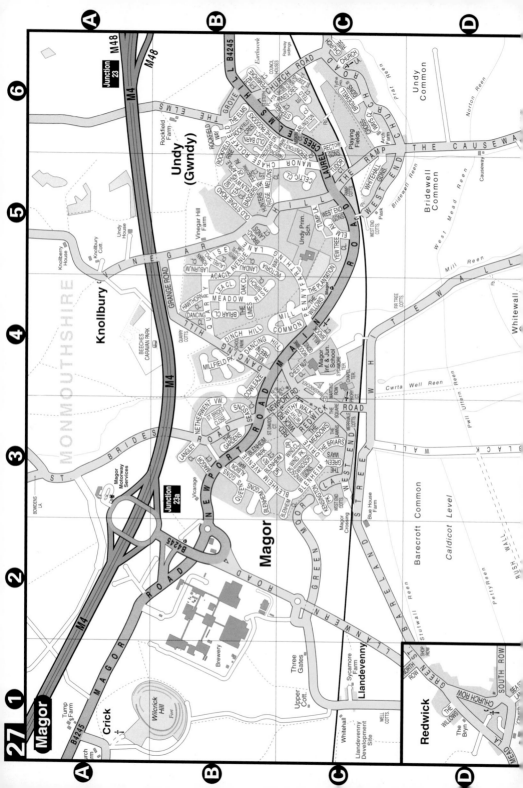

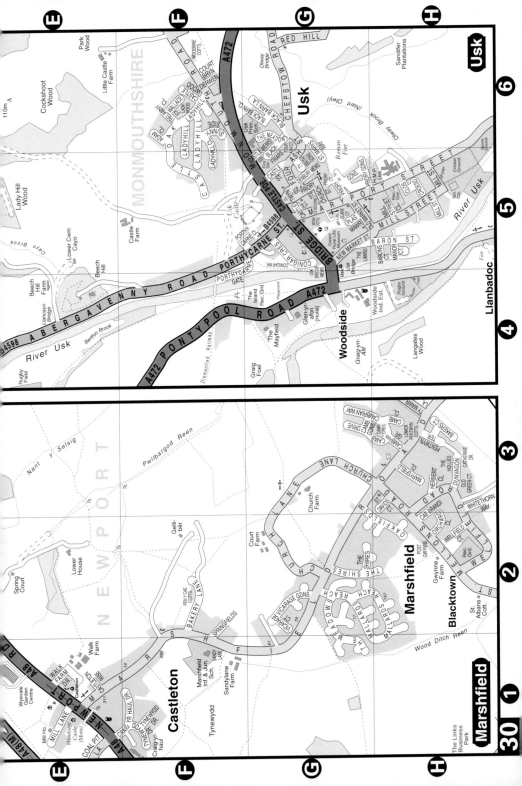

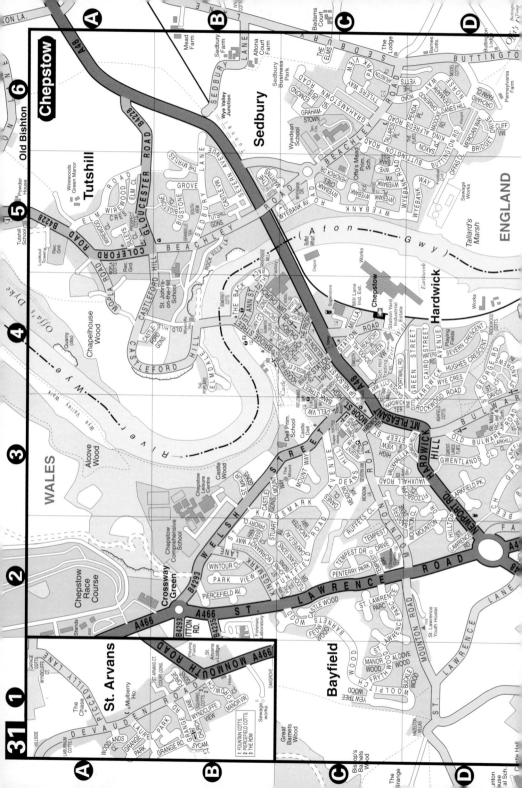

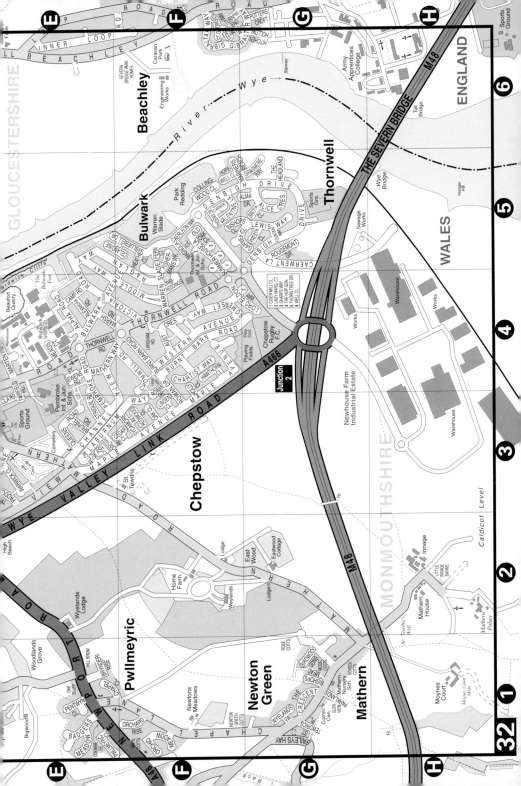

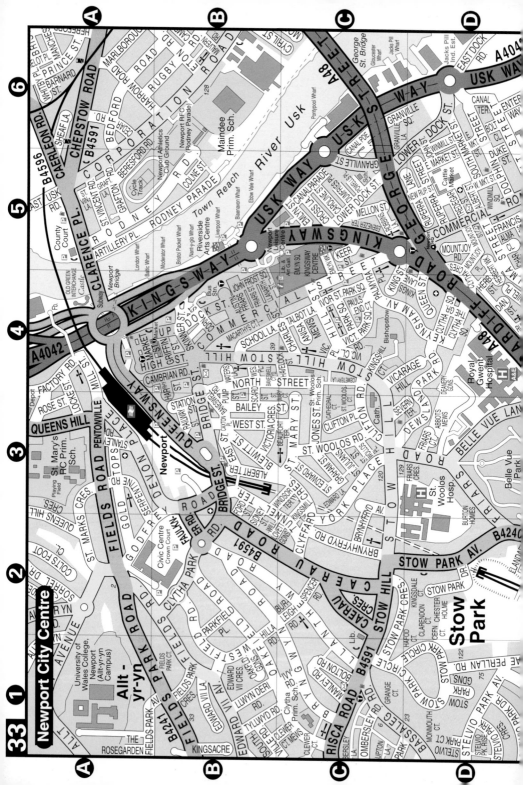

INDEX Abbreviations used

Allot(s).	Allotment(s)	Coll.	College	Fld(s).	Field(s)	Inf.	Infant	Off(s).	Office(s)	S.	South
Amb.	Ambulance	Comm.	Community	Flts.	Flats	Junc.	Junction	Orch(s).	Orchard(s)	Sq.	Square
App.	Approach	Comp.	Comprehensive	Fb(s).	Footbridge(s)	Jun.	Junior	Par.	Parade	Stn.	Station
Arc.	Arcade	Cov.	Covered	Gdns.	Gardens	La.	Lane	Pk.	Park	St.	Street
Av.	Avenue	Crn.	Corner	Gt.	Great	Lib.	Library	Pass.	Passage	Ten.	Tennis
Br.	Bridge	Cott(s).	Cottage(s)	Gra.	Grange	Lit.	Little	Pav.	Pavilion	Ter.	Terrace
Brd.	Broad	Cres.	Crescent	Grn.	Green	Lwr.	Lower	Pl.	Place	Up.	Upper
Bldg(s).	Building(s)	Cft.	Croft	Grd.	Ground	Mkt.	Market	Pr.	Precinct	Vic.	Vicarage
Bung(s).	Bungalow(s)	Ct.	Court	Gr.	Grove	Mag.	Magistrates	Prim.	Primary	Vw.	View
Bus.	Business	Dis.	Disused	Hd.	Head	Mdw(s).	Meadow(s)	Rec.	Recreation	Vlls.	Villas
Cara.	Caravan	Dr.	Drive	Hts.	Heights	Mem.	Memorial	Res.	Reservoir	Wk.	Walk
Cem.	Cemetery	E.	East	Hosp.	Hospital	Mon.	Monument	Resid.	Residential	Wy.	Way
Cen.	Centre	Ent.	Enterprise	Ho.	House	Mt.	Mount	Rd.	Road	W.	West
Cl.	Close	Est.	Estate	Ind.	Industrial	N.	North	Sch.	School	Yd.	Yard

Use of this Index: An alphabetical order is followed.

1. Each street name is followed by a map reference giving a page number and coordinates: Abbey Cottages **10** H4.

2. Names not appearing on the map are shown with an * and the reference of the nearest adjoining street:
Back Club Row*, High St. **2** H1.

3. Where a street name appears more than once the reference is given: Caerphilly Road **17** B1/C5.

4. There is insufficient space to name all streets in situ, these appear in numbered lists and the reference is given:
David Walk (3) **17** A4.

5. House numbers along streets are shown: *250.*

A

Abbey Cottages **10** H4
Abbey Farm Lane **10** H4
Abbey Green **10** G2
Abbey Grove **10** H4
Abbey Road (Cwmbran) **10** E1
Abbey Road (Newport) **16** H6
Abbots Mews **33** D3
Abergavenny Road (Blaenavon)
....**1** B4
Abergavenny Road (Penperlleni)
....**5** A5
Abergavenny Road (Usk) ..**30** E4
Abergelli Cottages.............**4** F1
Aberthaw Avenue **21** A5
Aberthaw Circle.................**21** A4
Aberthaw Close.................**21** A5
Aberthaw Drive **21** A4
Aberthaw Road **21** A4/A6
Acacia Avenue (Newport) ..**21** A4
Acacia Avenue (Undy) **27** B5
Acacia Square...................**21** A4
Acer Way **12** H1
Acorn Close (Abersychan) ..**3** B2
Acorn Close (Rogerstone) **12** G3
Adam Close **30** F6
Adelaide Street..................**14** G5
Adeline Street **19** D5
Adit Walk..........................**7** B5
Adrian Boult Green **21** B5
Ael y Bryn **1** B5
Aerons House **8** F5
Afon Close **6** E4
Afon Court.........................**3** B3
Afon Gardens **15** A2
Afon Llwyd Terrace (18) **3** D3
Afon Llwyd Close...............**15** D4
Afon Mead **12** G1
Afon Terrace.....................**9** C3
Agincourt Street **14** G5
Ailesbury Street **14** G5
Alan Close (1) **17** A4

Alanbrooke Avenue **13** B3
Albany Street **14** G5
Albert Avenue **16** H1
Albert Court......................**16** H1
Albert Road.......................**2** H1
Albert Street **33** D5
Albert Terrace **33** B3
Albion Close **19** C5
Albion Court (Caldicot) **28** G5
Albion Court (Newport) **19** C6
Albion House.....................**28** G5
Albion Place **4** E3
Albion Road **4** G4
Albion Square **31** C3
Albion Street **19** C5
Albion Way **27** B3
Alcock Close.....................**21** C3
Alcove Wood.....................**31** C1
Alder Close **5** D4
Alder Grove.......................**13** D4
Alderney Street.................**14** G5
Alders, The **10** F4
Alexandra Court*, Alexandra Rd.
....**19** D6
Alexandra Lane*, Alexandra Rd.
....**19** D6
Alexandra Road (Chepstow)
....**32** E4
Alexandra Road (Newport) **19** D6
Alexandra Road (Pontypool)
....**6** G2
Alfred Street **14** H6
Alianore Road...................**28** G5
Alice Crescent **32** G5
Alice Street **19** D5
Allen Close **12** E6
Alleyn House (1) **9** C4
Allgood Avenue.................**1** C3
Allt yr Yn Avenue **33** A1
Allt yr Yn Close **33** A1
Allt yr Yn Court **14** G3
Allt yr Yn Crescent **14** G3
Allt yr Yn Heights **14** H3

Allt yr Yn Road **33** A2
Allt yr Yn View..................**14** H2
Allt yr Yn Way **14** G3
Alma Close **33** D5
Alma Drive **32** G5
Alma Place **6** G2
Alma Street (Blaenavon) **1** B4
Alma Street (Newport) **33** D4
Almond Court*, Larch Grove
....**13** C4
Almond Drive **13** C3
Alpha Road **32** E4
Alpine Cottages **4** F3
Alton Terrace **4** E5
Alway Close **21** A5
Alway Crescent **21** A5
Alway Parade **21** A5
Alwyn Close **12** G4
Amberley Place **4** E4
Ambleside Lower **2** H1
Ambleside Upper **2** H2
Ambrose Way **5** D4
Ambryn Road **5** D5
Amroth Walk **8** E6
Amy Johnson Close **21** C3
Anderson Close **19** D3
Anderson Place **13** C3
Aneurin Bevan Court (Newport)
....**20** G1
Aneurin Bevan Court (Pontypool)
....**4** G5
Angiddy Close...................**28** E5
Anglesey Court **15** C2
Anisa Mews **33** C4
Anne Street.......................**1** B4
Annesley Road **16** G1
Anson Green.....................**23** B1
Anthony Drive **15** C2
Anwyll Close **15** C3
Apple Avenue **27** B5
Apprentice Close...............**32** F6
Aragon House*, Oakfield Road
....**19** A3

Aragon Street **14** G5
Aran Court..........................**7** B5
Arcade, The (Cwmbran) **9** D2
Arcade, The (Parc-Seymour)
....**24** E6
Arcadia Way **3** C5
Archer Road **7** D5
Archibald Street **21** A1
Archway Court*, Moor St. ..**31** C3
Argosy Way.......................**21** B1
Argyle Street.....................**14** G5
Arlington Close (Newport)..**13** C3
Arlington Close (Undy) **27** C6
Arlington Court **31** C6
Armstrong Close **21** B4
Arne Close **23** D1
Arnold Close **19** C2
Arthur Bliss Road **21** B5
Arthur Close **19** C5
Arthur Street (Caerleon) ...**15** D4
Arthur Street (Newport).....**19** C5
Arthurs Court **29** C2
Artillery Place **33** A5
Arundel Close (1) **7** D4
Arundel Road **21** A2
Ash Close **32** E3
Ash Green **10** G2
Ash Grove (Caldicot).........**28** F4
Ash Grove (Cwmbran) **9** C2
Ash Grove (Pontypool) **3** D6
Ash Grove (Underwood)....**23** D6
Ash Tree Road **26** G2
Ashdown Court*,
   Commercial Road **19** C6
Ashfield Cottages **31** D3
Ashfield House*, Mt. Pleasant
....**31** D3
Ashfield Houses*, Cross St. **1** C4
Ashford Close **9** C4
Ashford Close North **9** C4
Ashford Close South..........**9** C4
Ashgrove Close..................**6** F1
Ashleigh Court...................**8** F3

Ashley Road 21 A3
Ashton House 8 E6
Ashwell 16 F5
Ashwell Cottages*, Ashwell
....16 F5
Ashwell Villas 16 F5
Aspen Way 13 C4
Asquith Street 6 E2
Aston Crescent 14 F4
Aubrey Hames Close 19 C3
Auckland Road 17 C6
Augustan Close 15 D2
Augustan Drive 15 D2
Augustan Way 15 D2
Augustus John Close 16 F3
Augustus Place 23 B1
Aust Crescent 32 F4
Austin Friars 33 B4
Austin Road 6 G2
Avalon Court 4 F4
Avalon Drive 16 G2
Avenue, The (Caldicot)......28 G4
Avenue, The (Coedkernew)18 F5
Avenue, The (Garndiffaith) ..2 G1
Avenue, The (New Inn).......5 C3
Avenue, The (Sebastopol)
....6 F1/G1
Avenue, The*, Bushy Park ..4 F4
Avenue, The*, Clytha Sq. ..19 B5
Avon Close (Caldicot) 28 E4
Avon Close (Newport).......14 E1
Avon Place 10 E3
Avon Road 1 C4
Avondale..............................1 C4
Avondale Close....................9 A2
Avondale Crescent 9 A2
Avondale Road ...6 G3/H3/9 A1
Avondale Way 9 A2

B

Back Club Row*, High St.....2 H1
Back, The 31 B4
Backhall Street 15 D4
Bacon Place 13 C3
Badgers Dene 31 D3
Badgers Meadow (Chepstow)
....32 E1
Badgers Meadow (Ponthir) 15 A5
Badgers Mede 7 D5
Badgers Walk 27 B5
Badgers Wood Close 17 D2
Badminton Road 16 F2
Badminton Villas 31 B4
Bagley Court 7 B4
Bailey Crescent 2 G2
Bailey Street (Garndiffaith) ..2 G1
Bailey Street (Newport).....33 B3
Baileys Hay.......................32 G1
Baileys Houses (1) 3 D2
Baileys Terrace (2) 3 D3
Baird Close 13 C2
Baker Street House (9).......1 D4
Bakers Court......................30 H3
Bakery Houses (Garndiffaith)
....2 G1

Bakery Houses*, New Rd. ..3 A3
Bakery Lane 30 F2
Bala Drive..........................12 G4
Bala House 8 E5
Balance Meadow..................2 F1
Balance Road 2 F1
Baldwin Close....................19 D5
Baldwin Street...................19 C5
Balfe Road 21 A6
Balmond Terrace 4 E4
Balmoral Lane 21 A3
Balmoral Road 21 A3
Baltic Terrace 10 H1
Bamber House (2) 9 C4
Baneswell Courtyard.........33 B4
Baneswell Road 33 B3
Bank Lane 16 F1
Bank Square 31 C4
Bank Street (Chepstow) 31 C3
Bank Street (Newport).......16 F1
Bankers Row........................1 A3
Bantock Close....................21 A6
Banwell Court 7 B4
Barbirolli Green 21 B5
Bardsey Close 16 G2
Bareland Street..................27 C2
Barn Close 3 C4
Barn Owl Road 28 G1
Barnard Street....................33 A4
Barnets 7 D4
Barnets Wood....................31 C2
Barnfield (Blaenavon) 1 C3
Barnfield (Ponthir) 15 A2/B6
Barnfield Close 24 F2
Barnfield Place 7 B6
Barnfield Terrace 1 C3
Baron Street 30 H5
Barons Court......................27 C5
Barons Court......................30 H5
Barrack Hill 14 G3
Barrie Gardens 19 D1
Barry Walk 12 G4
Barthropp Street 21 B3
Bassaleg Road 33 D1
Batchelor Road 21 A2
Batchelors Row....................2 H2
Bath Green 10 E4
Bath Street 14 H6
Bay Tree Close 15 D1
Beachley Road (Beachley) 32 E6
Beachley Road (Sedbury)
....31 B5/C5
Beacons Close 12 G4
Beatty Road 23 B1
Beaufort Close 8 F5
Beaufort Place (Chepstow)
....31 C4
Beaufort Place (Newport) ..16 F2
Beaufort Road 16 F2
Beaufort Square 31 C4
Beaufort Terrace 33 C3
Beaumaris Close................17 B2
Beaumaris Drive 10 E4
Beaumaris House 10 E4
Beddick 7 D4

Bedford Close (2) 7 D4
Bedford Road 33 A6
Beech Close (Cwmbran) 7 B6
Beech Close (Underwood) 23 D5
Beech Grove (Chepstow) ..31 D3
Beech Grove (Newport) ...20 F2
Beech Road (Caldicot) 28 F4
Beech Road (Pontypool) 6 G1
Beech Tree Terrace 3 D3
Beecham Street 21 A6
Beechcroft Road 16 H3
Beechdale Road 16 H3
Beeches Caravan Park 27 A4
Beeches Road 3 C4
Beeches, The (Blaenavon) ..1 B3
Beeches, The (Cwmbran)..10 E1
Beeches, The (Pontypool) ..3 C3
Beeches, The*, Beech Grove
....20 F2
Beechfield Avenue 16 H3
Beechleigh Close 7 D3
Beechwood Crescent 21 A3
Beechwood Road....16 H3/21 A3
Beechwood Walk 3 C4
Belgrave Court (21) 3 D3
Bell Lane 3 B2
Belle Vue Close (Cwmbran)
....10 E1
Belle Vue Close (Pontypool)
....3 C4
Belle Vue Cottages 7 B4
Belle Vue Court (11) 3 D3
Belle Vue Lane 33 D3
Belle Vue Road 10 F1
Belle Vue Terrace (Cwmbran)
....8 F2
Belle Vue Terrace (Newport)
....19 C5
Bellevue Gardens*, Abbey Road
....10 E1
Bellin Close.......................15 C3
Belmont Hill 16 F5
Belmont House 16 F6
Belvedere Terrace 14 G4
Ben Jonson Way...............19 C1
Benbow Road 23 B1
Bencroft Lane 28 E1
Benson Avenue (2) 17 A4
Bentley Close 12 G3
Benton Villas*, Commercial Cl.
....2 H1
Beresford Road..................33 A5
Berkeley Court 7 C4
Berkley Close 17 B3
Berkley Crescent 6 G2
Berkley Road 17 B3
Berthin 7 D5
Berthon Road 6 H5
Bessemer Close 13 C2
Bethel Court (1) 2 G1
Bethel Lane..........................7 A4
Bethesda Close 12 H3
Bethesda Place 12 H3
Betjeman Avenue 28 H4
Bettws Close 14 E2

Bettws Hill.................12 E6/14 E1
Bettws Lane 14 E2
Bettws Shopping Centre....13 D1
Betwyns (1).........................8 F5
Bevans Lane........................6 H2
Bideford Close 19 D3
Bideford Road....................19 D3
Bigham Row 4 H5
Bigstone Close 31 B5
Bigstone Grove 31 B5
Bilston Street.....................21 B2
Birbeck Road.....................28 F3
Birch Close 27 B4
Birch Grove (Cwmbran) 8 G3
Birch Grove (Rogerstone)..12 H3
Birch Grove (Underwood)
....23 C6/D6
Birch Hill 13 D4
Birch Trees 17 C4
Birches, The 7 C5
Birchgrove Close 13 D4
Birchwood Houses*,
Freeholdland Road 3 C3
Birdwood Gardens 32 G1
Bishop Close (Caerwent) ..26 H3
Bishop Street 14 H6
Bishops Close (Chepstow) 32 F5
Bishops Mead....................32 G1
Bishpool Estate..................16 H6
Bishpool Lane 16 H6
Bishton Lane 31 A6
Bishton Street 21 A1
Black Ash Path 16 F5
Black Barn Close 30 G6
Black Barn Lane 30 G6
Black Friars........................30 G5
Black Horse Lane*,
Somerton Road 21 B3
Black Lane 1 B4
Black Path............................2 H2
Black Rock Road 29 B4
Black Wall 27 C4
Blackbird Close (Newport) 13 B3
Blackbird Road 28 G5
Blackbirds Close (Rogerstone)
....17 B5
Blackett Avenue 13 D3
Blacksmith Lane 26 F5
Blacksmiths Way 18 G4
Blackthorn Grove 15 D1
Blackwater Close 11 D6
Blaen y Cwm View 8 F2
Blaen y Pant Avenue 14 F3
Blaen y Pant Crescent 14 F3
Blaen y Pant House 14 F3
Blaen y Pant Place 14 F3
Blaendare Farm Road 4 H4
Blaendare Road 4 H4
Blaenwern 9 B2
Blake Road 21 B4
Blanch Close 20 G2
Blenheim Avenue 27 C3
Blenheim Close..................27 C3
Blenheim Court (Cwmbran) 8 E5
Blenheim Court (Magor) ..27 B3

Blenheim Drive 27 B3
Blenheim Gardens 27 B3
Blenheim Park...................27 B3
Blenheim Road (Cwmbran)..8 E5
Blenheim Road (Newport).21 A3
Blenheim Square*, Blenheim Rd.
....8 E5
Bleriot Close 21 C3
Blethyn Close 26 E6
Blewitt Street....................33 B3
Blodwen Road 5 D4
Blodwen Way 5 D4
Bloomfield Close..............16 H6
Blorange Terrace 1 A4
Blossom Close 23 A3
Blue Boar 3 A1
Bluebell Court 8 E2
Bluebell Drive 32 F5
Bluebell Way.....................12 G1
Bluetts Houses*, Viaduct Road
....2 H2
Bluetts Lane*, Bluetts Rd.....2 H1
Bluetts Road 2 H1
Boddington Terrace (1).......15 D4
Bolt Close 33 D6
Bolt Street 33 D5
Bolton Road 33 C1
Bolton Street.....................14 G4
Bolts Row*, Chepstow Rd. 21 A4
Bond Street.......................14 H5
Boot Lane*, Broad Street 1 C4
Booths Lane 3 D1
Boswell Close 19 C2
Bosworth Drive 14 G4
Bowdens Lane 24 F6/27 A3
Bowen Close........................1 B4
Bowen Place*, Francis Drive
....19 C5
Bowleaze 7 D5
Box Tree Close 15 D1
Boyle Close.......................13 D2
Brades, The 15 C4
Brain Close 23 C2
Bramble Way 24 H5
Bramley Close...................23 A4
Brangwyn Avenue 10 G3
Brangwyn Crescent 16 G2
Brankleys Houses...............1 C6
Brassknocker Street 27 C4
Brechfa Close 15 A5
Brecon Court.....................15 C2
Brecon Road......................16 G2
Brecon Walk 9 D2
Briar Close 27 B4
Briars, The 27 C3
Brick Houses*, Avon Road ..1 C4
Brick Yard Lane 17 A6
Brickyard Cottages 7 A4
Bridewell Gardens 27 C6
Bridge Buildings*, Godfrey Road
....19 A4
Bridge Street (Blaenavon) ..1 C4
Bridge Street (Chepstow) ..31 B4
Bridge Street (Newport) 19 A4
Bridge Street (Pontypool) 6 E2

Bridge Street (Usk) 30 G5
Bridge Terrace 17 C5
Bridget Drive 31 D6
Briers Gate 8 G2
Brightstown........................2 G1
Bristol House 3 D3
Bristol Street.....................33 A6
Bristol View Close...............7 D3
British School Close 3 A1
Briton Close (Chepstow)....32 G5
Britten Close (Newport).....21 B5
Broad Quay Road 22 E1
Broad Street (Abersychan) ..3 B3
Broad Street (Blaenavon) 1 C4
Broad Street (Newport) 2 A4
Broad Street (Pontypool) 6 E2
Broad View 7 B5
Broadcommon Close 21 C5
Broadlands Court 27 B5
Broadmead Park................21 B5
Broadstreet Common 22 F5
Broadwalk 15 D4
Broadwater Road 21 D5
Broadway (Caerleon) 16 E4
Broadway (Pontypool) 4 F5
Broadweir Road 10 E1
Broadwell Court 15 D4
Broadwood Close 23 D1
Brodawel House*, Mill St. ..15 D4
Bron y Garth*, The Highway
....9 C4
Bronllys Place 9 C3
Bronte Grove 19 D1
Brook Street 9 A2
Brookfield Close 21 B4
Brooklands House*, New Street
....9 B1
Brooklands Terrace.............9 B1
Brooklea 15 C3
Brookside (Blaenavon) 1 B4
Brookside (Caldicot)..........28 E4
Brookside (Cwmbran) 8 E5
Brookside (Newport) 13 D1
Brookside Estate 8 G4
Broom Close 12 H2
Broome Path 8 E5
Brown Close 21 C3
Browning Close.................19 C2
Brunel Avenue 12 H4
Brunel Road (Chepstow)....32 E3
Brunel Road (Cwmbran) 8 E4
Brunel Street 19 D6
Brunswick Court (14) 3 D3
Brutes Row 1 C3
Bryn Bevan 14 F4
Bryn Carreg 2 H2
Bryn Cottages 32 F1
Bryn Eglwys 9 C3
Bryn Garw..........................9 C3
Bryn Gomer 9 A3
Bryn Gwyn Place.................4 F4
Bryn Gwyn Road...............33 C1
Bryn Hedydd 17 C2
Bryn Milwr 8 G6
Bryn Onnen Court...............8 G3

Bryn Rhedyn.....................10 G5
Bryn Terrace (3) (Pontypool)
....3 D3
Bryn Terrace (Blaenavon)....1 B4
Bryn Terrace (Garndiffaith)..2 G1
Bryn Welon Close 1 C5
Bryn, The 13 C1
Brynavon 1 C4
Bryncelyn Place 7 B6
Bryncelyn Road...................7 B6
Brynderi Rise 32 E1
Brynderwen Cottages 3 A3
Brynderwen Court..............16 H1
Brynderwen Grove 16 H1
Brynderwen Road 16 H1
Brynglas 8 G5
Brynglas & Malpas Relief Road
....13 B3
Brynglas Avenue 14 F4
Brynglas Close 14 E4
Brynglas Court 14 E4
Brynglas Crescent 14 F4
Brynglas Drive...................14 H2
Brynglas Gardens*, Brynglas Rd.
....14 G4
Brynglas Road 14 G4
Bryngwyn Road.................19 B3
Brynheulog 4 H6/5 D1
Brynhyfryd..........................9 B4
Brynhyfryd Avenue 33 C2
Brynhyfryd Close 6 H5
Brynhyfryd Road................33 C2
Brynhyfryd Terrace 3 C2
Brynteg 3 B2
Brynteg Place 6 G6
Brynwern 4 F4
Buchan Close 19 C2
Buchanan Way 18 G5
Buckingham Crescent........16 H2
Buckingham Place 16 H2
Buckland Close 28 G1
Buckle Wood.....................31 D1
Budden Crescent 28 F5
Builth Close.......................20 H6
Buller Street 4 E2
Bulmore Road 16 F5
Bulwark Avenue 32 E4
Bulwark Road 31 D3
Bungalows, The 1 A3
Burberry Close 12 G1
Burford Street 1 B4
Burleigh Road....................33 C2
Burnfort Road 19 C2
Burns Close 19 D1
Burns Crescent 28 G3
Burns Lane 8 E6
Burnt Barn Road 32 F4
Burton Homes (Caerwent) 26 G3
Burton Homes (Newport) ..33 D2
Burton Road 16 F2
Burton Villas 26 G3
Bush Lane 4 G4
Bushy Park 4 F4
Butlers Court (2) 2 G1
Butlers Lane (3) 2 G1

Butlers Row........................3 B2
Buttercup Close 12 G1
Buttercup Court 8 F2
Buttermere Way 16 F2
Butterworth Close 23 C1
Buttington Cottages 31 D6
Buttington Hill 31 D6
Buttington Road 31 D5
Buttington Terrace 31 D6
Buxton Close 19 D3
Byrde Close 21 A5
Byron Place (Caldicot) 28 G4
Byron Place (Cwmbran) 8 E6
Byron Road........................19 C2
Bythway Road.....................3 C5
Byways 7 D4/8 E4

C Row................................1 C2
Caban Close 12 G4
Cadoc Close 26 H3
Cadoc Road 7 B5
Cae Brandi 30 H2
Cae Brynton Road 19 C3
Cae Derwen 10 F1
Cae Mawr Avenue.............28 F4
Cae Mawr Grove 28 G4
Cae Mawr Road 28 F4
Cae Melin 6 G6
Cae Perllan Road 33 D1
Cae Rhedyn 9 C4
Cae White 1 B3
Cae yr Ebol 9 C1
Caepalish 3 D3
Caepalish Place (9) 3 D3
Caerau Cottages 26 F5
Caerau Crescent 33 C2
Caerau Road 33 C2
Caerleon House (Newport) 18 F5
Caerleon Houses*, High Street
....15 D4
Caerleon Road (Llanfrechfa)
....10 E4
Caerleon Road (Newport) ..33 A5
Caerleon Road (Ponthir)
.................................15 A2/A5
Caerleon Way 32 F5
Caerlicken Lane 24 E3
Caernarvon Close 9 D4
Caernarvon Crescent
.............................9 D3/10 E3
Caernarvon Drive 17 B2
Caerphilly Close 17 C2
Caerphilly Road............17 B1/C5
Caerwent Brook Cottages..26 H4
Caerwent Gardens 26 G3
Caerwent Lane 32 G5
Caerwent Road (Cwmbran) 9 A3
Caerwent Road (Pontypool) 3 D6
Caesar Crescent................15 C2
Caird Street.......................31 D4
Calcot House (3) 9 C4
Caldicot Bypass 28 G4
Caldicot Road (Caldicot)
.............................28 E1/E5

Caldicot Road (Portskewett) 29 B1
Caldicot Road (Rogiet) 28 G1
Caldicot Street 21 B2
Caldicot Way......................9 B2
Caldy Close 16 G2
Cam Court...........................7 B4
Cambria Close 15 D5
Cambria Street 6 F2
Cambrian Centre*, Queensway
....19 A4
Cambrian Close 30 H3
Cambrian Crescent...........30 H3
Cambrian Drive.................30 H3
Cambrian Gardens 30 G3
Cambrian Grove................30 H3
Cambrian Road.................19 A5
Cambrian Way 30 H3
Cambridge Court 15 C1
Cambridge Road...............19 A6
Camellia Avenue 12 G1
Camelot Court...................15 D5
Camelot Place 14 H6
Camp Road (Chepstow) ...32 E4
Camp Road (Sudbrook) 29 D4
Campanula Drive 12 G1
Campbell Street 4 E4
Camperdown Road...........21 B3
Campion Close (Cwmbran) 8 G3
Campion Close (Newport) 14 H4
Camrose Walk 8 E6
Canal Bank (Newport) 13 C2
Canal Bank*, Blaen y Pant Cres.
....14 F3
Canal Bank*, Osborne Road
....4 E5
Canal Close........................6 F2
Canal Parade 33 C5/C6
Canal Side 10 E1
Canal Street 14 G4
Canal Terrace....................33 D6
Canberra Close...................8 E6
Canberra Crescent 19 B1
Candwr Lane 15 A2/A6
Candwr Park 15 A6
Candwr Road..............15 A2/B6
Canford Close.....................3 C4
Canon Lane 26 H3
Canon Street.....................14 H6
Canterbury Close (1) 14 H5
Canterbury Way 29 C3
Cantref Close 12 G4
Capel Close 19 C6
Capel Court (23) 3 D3
Capel Crescent 19 C5
Capel Ed Lane 5 A5
Capel Newydd Avenue 1 C5
Capel Newydd Road...........1 C4
Capel Street (Newport) 19 C5
Capel Street (Pontypool) 4 G5
Caper Court 24 H2
Caradoc Road.....................9 C1
Caradoc Street 3 B2
Caradoc Walk 1 B4
Caradog Close 15 C3

Cardiff Road
....18 E6/19 D2/20 E1/33 D4
Cardigan Close 9 B3
Cardigan Court 15 C2
Cardigan Crescent 9 A3
Cardigan Place 16 G2
Carey Road.......................21 A3
Carfax Path (2) 8 F5
Carisbrooke Road............21 A2
Carlisle Street 19 D6
Carlton Court (15) 3 D3
Carlton Road 16 G1
Carlton Terrace.................16 E4
Caroline Road....................5 D4
Caroline Street 33 C5
Caroline Way 5 D4
Carpenter Close 24 H2
Carpenters Arms Lane*, High St.
....19 A5
Cartwright Green 13 D3
Cas Troggy 28 E4
Cas Troggy Road 25 A4
Castell y Bwch Cottages ...11 A4
Castle Close 17 B5
Castle Coch Drive............20 H1
Castle Court (Cwmbran) 8 G3
Castle Court (Newport) 17 B5
Castle Court (Portskewett) 29 B2
Castle Court (Usk) 30 G5
Castle Court*, Welsh St. ...31 B2
Castle Gardens (Caldicot)..28 E5
Castle Gardens (Chepstow)
....31 B3
Castle Lane......................16 E5
Castle Lea........................28 F6
Castle Lodge Close 28 G6
Castle Lodge Crescent 28 G6
Castle Mews (Caerleon) ...16 E5
Castle Mews (Usk) 30 G5
Castle Mews*, George Street
....4 F5
Castle Oak 30 F5
Castle Parade...................30 G5
Castle Park Close 19 C1
Castle Park Road 19 C1
Castle Rise 25 B3
Castle Street (Blaenavon) ...1 B4
Castle Street (Caerleon) ...16 E5
Castle Street (Newport) 19 C6
Castle Street (Usk) 30 G5
Castle View.......................31 B5
Castle Way 29 C1
Castle Wood 30 F6
Castle Wood 31 C2
Castleford Gardens..........31 A4
Castleford Hill 31 A4
Castleton Rise..................30 E1
Castlewood (Talywain) 2 H1
Caswell Way 21 D3
Catalpa Close 13 C4
Cathedral Court 33 C3
Catherine Close 20 G2
Catherine Cottages 24 F2
Catherine Drive.................30 H3
Catref Melus 21 B3

Catsash Road (Langstone)
....23 A4
Catsash Road (Newport) ..16 G6
Causeway Cottages 27 D6
Causeway, The.................27 D6
Caxton Place....................33 B3
Cecil Lane 17 A4
Cecil Sharpe Road 23 C2
Cedar Close 32 F3
Cedar Court 18 G4
Cedar Road......................33 A6
Cedar Walk 7 B5
Cedar Wood Close 12 G1
Cedar Wood Drive 12 G1
Cedars, The 23 C6
Cefn Close (Cwmbran) 9 B4
Cefn Close (Newport) 12 H5
Cefn Court (Newport) 33 D2
Cefn Court (Rogerstone) ..12 H5
Cefn Drive........................12 H4
Cefn Milwr.........................8 G6
Cefn Rise 12 H3
Cefn Road...............12 G3/H4
Cefn Walk 12 H5
Cefn Wood 17 A4
Celandine Court (Chepstow)
....32 F5
Celandine Court (Cwmbran)
....8 E2
Celtic Close......................27 C5
Celtic Way 18 G5/H6
Celyn Court........................7 B5
Celynen Grove 20 E2
Cemetery Lane 33 C4
Cenfedd Street 14 G6
Central Avenue ...21 C5
Central Drive.......................3 C4
Central Mews*, Market St. ..4 F5
Central Way 7 B5
Centurion Court 26 G4
Centurion Gate 15 D5
Ceredig Court (1) 10 E4
Chadwick Close 13 D3
Chaffinch Way..................20 F2
Channel View (Chepstow) 32 E3
Channel View (Cwmbran) ...7 B5
Channel View (Newport)....17 C3
Channel View (Pontypool)
..............................4 E6/5 A1
Chapel Close (Chepstow)..32 E1
Chapel Close (Garndiffaith) 2 G1
Chapel Crescent*, Hanbury Rd.
....4 E3
Chapel Farm Lane 24 H5
Chapel Lane (Chepstow) ..32 F1
Chapel Lane (Cwmbran)......9 A3
Chapel Mead......................5 A5
Chapel Road.......................4 E2
Chapel Row........................1 B2
Chapel Street 9 C1
Chapel Terrace (Magor) 27 C4
Chapel Terrace (Newport) 17 B1
Chapel Terrace*, Hanbury Road
....4 E2
Chapman Close 13 C3

Chapman Court*, Penllyn Av.
....19 B2
Charles Street (Blaenavon) 1 C4
Charles Street (Cwmbran) ..9 B1
Charles Street (Newport) ..33 C4
Charles Street (Pontypool) ..6 E2
Charlesville 3 D3
Charlotte Green 19 C5
Charlotte Street.................33 D5
Charlotte Walk 19 C5
Charnwood House 8 E5
Charnwood Road 14 F6
Charston 7 D5
Chartist Drive 12 H4/17 A4
Chartist Tower*, Commercial St.
....33 B4
Chartist Way 32 F4
Chase, The 24 F1
Chaucer Close 28 G4
Chaucer Court*, Chaucer Road
....16 H2
Chaucer Road...................16 H2
Chelmer Close 12 E6
Chelmer Walk 12 E6
Chelston Place 14 G4
Chepstow Close 9 A3
Chepstow Rise 9 A3
Chepstow Road (Caldicot) 28 F5
Chepstow Road (Langstone)
.............................23 A3/24 G2
Chepstow Road (Newport)
.............................16 H4/21 A2/33 A5
Chepstow Road (Usk) 30 G6
Cheriton Path 8 E5
Cherry Tree Close (Caerleon)
....15 D4
Cherry Tree Close (Cwmbran)
....9 C4
Cherry Tree Close (Langstone)
....23 A4
Cherry Tree Close (Newport)
....13 D4
Cherwell Walk...................11 D6
Chester Close 5 C5
Chester Holme 33 D2
Chestnut Close (Magor) ...27 C4
Chestnut Close (Pontypool) 5 C5
Chestnut Cottages 6 F2
Chestnut Drive 28 G2
Chestnut Green...................7 B5
Chestnut Grove.................15 D1
Chichester Close...............16 E2
Chick Lane 19 B2
Chiltern Close (Newport) ..16 H5
Chiltern Close (Risca) 12 E1
Chirk Close 20 H6
Christchurch Hill 16 G6
Christchurch House*,
Chepstow Road...............23 B1
Christchurch Road ...16 H1/H3
Christina Crescent 17 B5
Church Avenue...................3 D5
Church Close (Caldicot) ...28 F6
Church Close (Cwmbran) ...9 C3
Church Close (Newport) 17 A5

Church Close (Pontypool) 6 F4
Church Cottages 16 E5
Church Crescent (Bassaleg)
................................17 C3
Church Crescent (Duffryn) 18 H4
Church Farm Close............14 E1
Church Lane (Marshfield) ..30 G2
Church Lane (New Inn)........6 E5
Church Lane (Newport) 18 H4
Church Lane (Pontypool) 3 D4
Church Lane (St. Arvans) ..31 A1
Church Lane (Undy)...........27 C6
Church Mews*, Lower Park Ter.
................................4 G5
Church Rise 27 C6
Church Road (Abersychan) 3 A1
Church Road (Blaenavon) ..1 B3
Church Road (Caldicot) 28 E5/F5
Church Road (Chepstow) ..31 C4
Church Road (Cwmbran) 7 B6
Church Road (Henllys) 8 E2
Church Road (Llanfrechfa) 10 G6
Church Road (Newport) 14 H6
Church Road (Talywain) 3 A1
Church Road (Undy)..........27 C6
Church Row (Chepstow) ..31 C4
Church Row (Redwick) 27 D1
Church Row (Sudbrook) ..29 D4
Church Row*, Church Rd....3 A1
Church Street (Caerleon) ..15 D4
Church Street (Newport) ..19 C6
Church Street (Rogerstone)
................................12 H2
Church Street (Usk) 30 G5
Church Terrace (4) (Pontypool)
................................3 D3
Church Terrace (Llanvaches)
................................25 B3
Church View 17 C5
Church View*, Church Road 1 B3
Churchfield Avenue............28 F5
Churchmead (Newport) 17 C5
Churchmeads (Caldicot) ..28 H1
Churchward Drive 21 B4
Churchwood 4 E5
Churchwood Close 4 E5
Churchwood Road 7 C6
Cider Mill Close (1) 32 F5
Cilgerran Court (2) 10 E4
Circle, The........................8 F6
Clapham Terrace 1 C2
Clare Court 30 G5
Clare Drew Way 9 B4
Claremont 13 C4
Clarence Court*, Caerleon Road
................................14 H6
Clarence Place (Newport) ..33 A4
Clarence Place (Pontypool)
................................4 G6/5 C1
Clarence Road 4 G5
Clarence Street (Newport) 19 C6
Clarence Street (Pontypool) 4 F5
Clarendon Close 32 F5
Clarendon Court 33 D2
Clarewain 6 E4

Clarewain Terrace.............6 E4
Clark Avenue 9 A1
Clawdd Du 10 H2
Clayton Street................14 H6
Clearview 26 F5
Clearwater Road 22 E6
Clearwell Court 17 C2
Cleaves Terrace 3 B2
Clement Atlee Drive 16 G6
Cleppa Park 18 F5
Clevedon Close 16 H2
Clevedon Road..............16 H2
Clewer Court..................33 C1
Clewer Court Mews 33 C1
Cliff View.......................31 D6
Clifton Place 33 C3
Clifton Road 33 C3
Clifton Square 6 E2
Clifton Street................12 F1
Clifton Terrace 1 B4
Clipper Close 16 E2
Clist Road 11 D5
Clist Walk 11 D6
Clomendy Road 10 E1
Clos Afon Llwyd 4 E5
Clos Aled....................28 E6
Clos Alwen 28 E5
Clos Croeso 30 H5
Clos Rheidol 28 E5
Close, The (Caldicot) 28 F4
Close, The (Cwmbran) ..10 G2
Close, The (Portskewett) ..29 C2
Clover Court 8 F2
Club Road 4 F3
Club Row (Abersychan) 3 C3
Club Row (Talywain).......2 H2
Clydach Close 14 E1/E2
Clyffard Crescent 33 C2
Clyffes.........................7 D4
Clytha Crescent 33 D4
Clytha Park Road 33 B2
Clytha Square..............33 D4
Co-op Terrace...............2 H1
Co-operative Flats 2 G1
Coal Pit Lane................30 E1
Cobb Crescent 28 G4
Cobner Close 3 D5
Coch y North Lane 17 D1
Coch y North Road........4 G1
Cocker Avenue 8 F6
Coed Cae 7 B6
Coed Cae Place 4 G5
Coed Cae Road 1 B4
Coed Camlas 5 C2
Coed Eithin Street........1 C4
Coed Eva Mill..............8 G5
Coed Garw 9 B3
Coed Glas.............8 F6/10 F1
Coed Lee......................8 F5
Coed Lee Court*, Coed Lee 8 F5
Coed Llwyd Close..........1 B5
Coed Melyn View*, Risca Road
................................33 C1
Coed Road 1 C4
Coed Terrace (Blaenavon) ..1 C5

Coed Terrace (Talywain) 3 A2
Coed y Canddo Road 5 C3
Coed y Gric 6 E2
Coed yr Eos 3 A3
Coedygraig Houses*, Station Rd.
................................6 E2
Coity Terrace 1 C2
Cold Bath Road 15 D4
Cold Store, The 10 F3
Coldra Interchange, The ..23 A2
Coldra Road 19 C3
Coldra Woods Drive
................................16 F6/23 A1
Coldra, The 23 B1
Coldstream Close 9 B3
Coleford Path 7 D5
Coleford Road 31 A2
Coleridge Green 8 E6
Coleridge Road..............21 A3
College Crescent 15 D4
College Glade 15 B3
College Road (Caerleon) ..15 C3
College Road (Pontypool)
................................4 E6/5 A1
College Terrace (6)..........3 D3
Collier Street..................14 H6
Collingwood Avenue 21 B3
Collingwood Close (Chepstow)
................................32 F5
Collingwood Close (Newport)
................................21 B3
Collingwood Crescent 21 B3
Collingwood Road............21 B3
Collins Close..................19 D1
Colne Street 33 B5
Colston Avenue 21 C2
Colston Court 21 B3
Colston Place 21 B3
Colts Foot Close 33 A1
Columbus House 23 A3
Comfrey Close 14 H3
Commercial Close 2 H1
Commercial Place..........9 B1
Commercial Road (Newport)
................................33 D5
Commercial Road (Talywain)
................................2 H1/3 A1
Commercial Street (5)
(Blaenavon) 1 C4
Commercial Street (Cwmbran)
................................10 E1
Commercial Street (Griffithstown)
................................6 E2
Commercial Street (Newport)
................................33 B4
Commercial Street (Pontnewydd)
................................9 B1
Commercial Street (Pontypool)
................................4 F5
Commercial Wharf 21 C1
Compton Close 12 H4
Conifer Close 15 D1
Conigar Crescent 30 G5
Conigar Walk 30 G5
Coniston Close 16 F1

Coniston House*, Blenheim Rd.
................................8 E5
Conrad House*, Beaufort Square
................................31 C4
Constable Drive..............16 F2
Constables Close 19 C6
Constance Street 14 G6
Conway Close.................9 C1
Conway Court 21 A3
Conway Croft 21 A3
Conway Road (Newport)....21 A2
Conway Road (Pontypool) ..4 F4
Conway Sac 21 A3
Conway Terrace 9 C3
Coolgreany Close 14 E3
Coolgreany Crescent 14 E3
Coomassie Street 19 D6
Coombe Lea 32 E1
Cooper Close 24 H2
Cooper Court 24 H2
Coopers Houses 3 C2
Copper Beech Close 15 D1
Coppins, The 13 D4
Corelli Street..................14 H6
Coriander Close 33 A1
Cork Road....................20 E6
Cormorant Way 20 G2
Corn Street 33 B4
Cornbrook Road 13 D1
Cornflower Close 12 G2
Cornwall Road 16 G1
Coronation Terrace (4)
(Pontypool) 3 D3
Coronation Terrace (Abersychan)
................................3 B3
Coronation Terrace (Talywain)
................................3 A2
Corporation Road
19 A6/21 A1/22 E2/F3/33 A5
Corris House 9 A2
Cory Park 10 H4
Cot Farm Circle..............23 C2
Cot Farm Close..............23 C2
Cot Farm Gardens 23 C2
Cot Farm Walk 23 C2
Cot Hill 23 C3
Cotman Close................16 G3
Cotswold Close..............16 H5
Cotswold Way (Newport) ..16 H5
Cotswold Way (Risca)........12 E1
Coulson Close 19 C5
Council Houses (Undy)....27 B6
Council Houses*, Manor Road
................................3 A1
Council Houses*, Wesley Street
................................10 E1
Court Bryn Derwen 30 F6
Court Cottages 28 E1
Court Crescent 17 C4
Court Farm Close 10 G3
Court Farm Road 10 G3
Court Gardens (Rogerstone)
................................12 H2
Court Gardens (St. Arvans) 31 B1
Court House Close 28 F5

Court House Road 25 A6
Court Meadow...............23 A4
Court Rise (4) 1 B4
Court Road 10 F2/F3
Court View 23 A5
Courtfield Close 12 H2
Courtlands, The 7 D4
Courtney Street................14 H6
Courtyard, The 18 G6
Courtybella Cottages*,
    Courtybella Gardens ..19 C6
Courtybella Gardens.......19 C6
Courtybella Terrace 19 C5
Coverack Road 21 B1
Covert Walk (3) 8 F4
Cowleaze 27 B4
Cowper Close 19 D1
Cowshed Lane 17 C3
Craig Ceiliog Lane
    ....8 H3/11 B3/C4
Craig yr Afon*, Wye Crescent
    ....31 D4
Craig yr Haul Drive 30 F1
Crane Street 4 F5
Crane Street Mews*, Crane St.
    ....4 F5
Cranham House 8 E6
Crawford Street................14 H6
Crescent Court 16 H2
Crescent Road 16 H2
Crescent, The (Cwmbran)....8 F6
Crescent, The (Mathern) ..32 G1
Cresswell Walk 7 D5
Criccieth Close 20 H1
Crick Road (Portskewett) ..29 B2
Crick Road (Shirenewton)..26 F5
Crindau Road 14 F4
Crocus Close 12 H1
Croes y Mwylach Roundabout
    ....13 B4
Croeswen 10 G2
Croesyceiliog Bypass 9 A4
Croft, The 24 F2
Crofton Mede 8 F4
Crofts Corner 7 D5
Cromwell Court 21 B3
Cromwell Place..................9 C1
Cromwell Road (Chepstow)
    ....32 F4
Cromwell Road (Newport)..21 B2
Cross Lane 33 C5
Cross Roads 7 B6
Cross Street (Blaenavon) ...1 C4
Cross Street (Caerleon) 16 E4
Cross Street (Garndiffaith) ..2 H1
Cross, The.......................28 F5
Crossfield Houses..............1 C4
Crossway 28 G1
Crossways Close 27 C6
Crouch Close 12 E6
Crown Close (Caerleon) ...15 D4
Crown Close (Cwmbran)......7 B6
Crown Rise 10 E4
Crown Road 10 G4
Crown Street....................16 H1

Croydon Close 16 F1
Croydon Court*, Croydon Close
    ....16 F1
Crumlin Road 4 H1
Crumlin Street....................4 G5
Cumberland Road............16 F1
Cunningham Road 23 B1
Curie Close 13 D3
Curlew Avenue 28 G5
Curlew Close 21 D6
Curwood 1 C3
Curzon Court....................21 A5
Cutter Close 16 E2
Cwm Cwddy Drive 17 C2
Cwm Cwddy Lane............17 C2
Cwm Cwddy Villas 17 C2
Cwm Dylan Close 17 C2
Cwm Farm Lane 4 H6
Cwm Lane 12 G4/H5
Cwm Sor Close..................5 D5
Cwm y Nant Fields 8 E6
Cwmavon Road (Abersychan)
    ....2 H3
Cwmavon Road (Blaenavon)
    ....1 C4
Cwmbran Drive
    ....6 H2/9 C1/10 F2/13 A2
Cwmffrdwr Cottages...........2 H3
Cwmffrwd Square 2 H3
Cwmffrwdoer 4 F1
Cwmnant Villas 10 E1
Cwmynyscoy Road 4 H5/5 D1
Cwr Drive 6 H2
Cwrdy Close 6 F1
Cwrdy Lane 6 F1
Cwrdy Road 6 F1
Cwrdy Walk 6 F1
Cwrt Bleddyn.....................8 F6
Cwrt Bleddyn Lane*, Cocker Av.
    ....8 F6
Cwrt Dowlais....................10 G1
Cwrt Glas 9 C4
Cwrt Morgan 26 G4
Cwrt Pencraig*, Caerau Cres.
    ....19 B3
Cwrt Severn 28 G3
Cypress Close 15 D1
Cyril Street 33 C6

D

D Row...............................1 C2
Daffodil Court 8 E3
Daffodil Lane 12 G1
Daffyn Court 2 G2
Daisy View 4 G6/5 C1
Dale Path 8 E4
Dale Road........................16 H5
Dancarga Drive 28 F5
Dancing Close..................27 B4
Dancing Hill.....................27 B4
Danes Close 31 C3
Danes Hill 31 D6
Daniel Place 33 D4
Daniel Street 33 D4
Danygraig 9 A3

Darby Close 12 H4
Darent Close....................12 E6
Darent Road 12 E6
Darent Walk 12 E6
Darlington Court 16 F1
Dart Road........................14 E1
Darwin Drive 13 D3
David Close 19 D5
David Walk (3) 17 A4
Davies Court (4) 2 G1
Davies Square 19 C5
Davis Close 4 E5
Davis Court 31 B4
Davis Larner Flats*, Walsall St.
    ....21 B1
Davy Close 13 D3
Dawson Close..................23 C2
Dean Court 8 G3
Dean Street......................16 H1
Deanery Gardens 33 D4
Deans Gardens................31 C2
Deans Hill 31 C3
Deepweir 28 G6
Deepweir Drive 28 G6
Deepweir Gardens 28 G6
Deer Park Lane................17 C5
Deerbrook 8 E4
Delius Close (Newport) 21 A5
Delius Close (Rogerstone) 12 G3
Dell View.........................31 C3
Delphinium Road 12 G1
Denbigh Drive 32 F5/G5
Denbigh Road 16 F1
Denbury Mews 30 G5
Dene Court (24) 3 D3
Denmark Drive 31 D6
Denny View 28 G6
Denton House (4) 9 C4
Dents Close 16 H6
Dents Hill 16 H6/21 A6
Derby Grove 21 C4
Derwent Court..................12 E5
Derwent House 8 E5
Devauden Road 31 A1
Devon Court 15 C2
Devon Place (Abersychan) ..3 A1
Devon Place (Newport).....33 B3
Dewberry Grove 12 F1
Dewsland Park Road 33 D3
Dewstow Close 28 F3
Dewstow Gardens............28 F4
Dewstow Road (Caerwent) 26 H3
Dewstow Road (Caldicot) ..28 E2
Dewstow Street................21 B2
Dibdin Close 23 D1
Dickens Drive 19 D1/D2
Dinas Path 8 E4
Dinch Hill 27 B4
Dingle Lane........................7 B6
Dingle Road 4 G6/5 C1
Dingle, The 20 E3
Dinham Road 26 G3
Ditch Hill 26 E5
Docks Way 19 D5/20 E2/E4
Dockwell Terrace 23 D3

Dolphin Court*, Commercial Rd.
    ....33 D5
Dolphin Street..................33 D5
Don Close 14 E1
Dorallt Close 8 F2
Dorallt Way 8 F2
Dorleigh Court....................7 B4
Dorset Close 21 C4
Dorset Crescent 21 C4
Dorstone Walk 10 E3
Dos Cottages*, Queens Hill
    ....14 H4
Dos Road 14 G4
Dowland Close 21 A6
Downing Street 21 B3
Downside Res. Home........23 D1
Drake Close 23 C1
Drayton Court 8 E6
Drill Hall Street*, Kemys St. 6 F2
Drinkwater Gardens 19 C2
Drovers Mews*, Tredegar Street
    ....33 D5
Drybrook Close 9 D2
Duckpool Lane 24 E6
Duckpool Road 16 G1
Dudley Street 21 B1
Duffryn Close 17 B3
Duffryn Drive 20 F1
Duffryn Lane 18 G5
Duffryn Shopping Centre ..20 G1
Duffryn Villas 15 A5
Duffryn Way 20 G1
Duke Street (Blaenavon) 1 B4
Duke Street (Newport) 33 D5
Dumfries Place 33 C5
Dunlin Avenue 28 G5
Dunn Square*, Alma St. ..19 C5
Dunnet Gardens 6 E5
Dunraven Drive................20 H6
Dunraven Road................10 E4
Dunstable Road 21 A6
Dunvagon 30 H3
Durand Road 28 G5
Durham Lane 14 G6
Durham Road 16 G1
Dyffryn Cottages*, Bluetts Road
    ....2 H1
Dyffryn Lane 18 G5
Dynevor Close 10 E4

E

E Row...............................1 C2
Eagle Close 28 G5
Earl Close 2 G1
Earl Street..........................2 H1
Earlsmede 8 E4
Earlswood Road 26 F5
East Avenue 6 G2
East Bank Road 22 E2
East Dock Cottages 22 F2
East Dock Road 21 C1/33 D6
East Grove Road 21 A4
East Lynne Gardens.........15 C4
East Market Street 33 D5
East Road.........................10 G2

East Roedin 8 G5
East Street 33 B3
East Usk Road 14 H5
East View (Abersychan) 3 A2
East View (Griffithstown).....6 F2
East View (Pontypool).........4 F5
East Way Road...................20 E6
Eastfield Close...................15 C3
Eastfield Drive....................15 B3
Eastfield Mews...................15 B3
Eastfield Road....................15 C3
Eastfield View 15 C3
Eastfield Way.....................15 C3
Eastgate Court*, Station Road
....15 D4
Eastgate Crescent 26 G3
Eastmoor Road..................21 C5
Eastway Road 22 F1/G1
Ebbw Road 28 E5
Ebenezer Drive..................17 A4
Ebenezer Terrace..............33 C5
Ebley Gardens...................29 C1
Ebury House (5) 9 C4
Edgecourt (4) 8 F4
Edgehill 10 F5
Edinburgh Close (3) 7 D4
Edison Ridge 13 C3
Edlogan Square 9 B3
Edlogan Villas.....................6 G2
Edlogan Way...................9 C2/C3
Edmond Road.....................31 C6
Edney View 20 F3
Edward German Crescent 23 C1
Edward Lane.......................33 C3
Edward Street (Griffithstown)
....6 E2
Edward Street (Pontypool) ..4 F4
Edward VII Avenue 33 B1
Edward VII Crescent..........33 B1
Edward VII Lane 33 B1
Edwin Street 14 G5
Eight Houses.......................3 B2
Eisteddfod Walk.................16 G6
Elaine Crescent 16 G2
Elan Close.........................14 E2
Elan Walk 8 E5
Elan Way............................28 E5
Elder Close 15 D2
Elgam Avenue 1 A4/B4
Elgam Green (1) 1 B4
Elgar Avenue 21 A5
Elgar Circle 21 A5
Elgar Close 21 A5
Elizabeth Sparks Close 28 G1
Elled Road 4 E4
Ellick Street 1 B4
Ellipse, The.........................6 G1
Ellwood Path 8 E5
Elm Avenue 27 C5
Elm Close (Chepstow).......31 A5
Elm Close (Pontypool) 3 C4
Elm Close (Underwood)......23 D5
Elm Grove (Newport) 13 D4
Elm Grove (Pontypool).......6 G2
Elm Hurst Close 3 C4

Elm Road (Caldicot) 28 F4
Elm Road (Chepstow)........31 A5
Elmdale 31 B4
Elms Hill 27 B6
Elms, The 31 C6
Elysia Street 14 G6
Emlyn Road 2 H1
Emlyn Square 33 C5
Emlyn Street 33 C5
Emlyn Terrace 2 H1
Emlyn Walk 33 C5
Empire Terrace....................2 G1
Endyings (5) 8 F5
Enfield Court*, Caerau Rd. 19 B3
Ennerdale Court 16 F2
Enterprise Way...................33 D6
Enville Close 19 B1
Enville Road 19 B1
Eric Coates Walk 21 A6
Eridge Road 2 H2
Eschol Close 21 B4
Eschol Court 21 B4
Esperanto Way...................21 D1
Essex Court 15 C3
Essex Street 21 A1
Estate Road 1 A2
Estuary Road 21 D5
Estuary View......................29 C1
Eton Road 33 B6
Evans Street 14 G5
Evesham Court...................14 G4
Eveswell Court 21 A1
Eveswell Lane*, Eveswell Street
....21 A2
Eveswell Park Road 16 H2
Eveswell Street 21 A2
Excelsior Close 21 B1
Exe Road 11 D6
Exeter Close 7 D4
Exeter Place 3 B2
Exeter Road 16 H1
Exeter Street 16 H1
Exmouth Place 31 C4

F

Factory Lane........................3 A2
Factory Road 33 A4
Fair Bank..............................1 B3
Fair View 31 D2
Fair View Terrace 2 H1
Fairfax Road 21 B3
Fairfield (Penperlleni) ...5 A5/B5
Fairfield (Talywain) 3 A2
Fairfield Close (Caerleon)..15 C2
Fairfield Close (Caldicot)...28 F3
Fairfield Road (Caerleon) ..15 C2
Fairfield Road (Chepstow) 32 E3
Fairfield Terrace 4 E3
Fairfields (Pontypool) 3 C3
Fairhill................................8 E4
Fairhill Walk 8 E4
Fairoak Avenue..................16 H1
Fairoak Court 16 H1
Fairoak Grove 17 C2
Fairoak Lane........................9 C4

Fairoak Mews 16 H1
Fairoak Terrace 16 H1
Fairview Court......................3 D4
Fairwater Close 8 E4
Fairwater Square Shops 8 F4
Fairwater Way 8 F4
Fairway Close 12 G3
Fairway,The 5 D4
Falcon Close......................28 G5
Fallowfield (6) 8 F5
Fallowfield Drive 21 C5
Faraday Close 13 D3
Farlays 8 F4
Farlow Walk 8 E6
Farm Hill 3 D4
Farm Lane (Newport) 16 G1
Farm Lane (Pontypool).......9 C2
Farm Road (British) 2 H1
Farm Road (Pontypool) 4 G5
Farmfield Lane 22 H6
Farmfield Road 22 H6
Farmwood Close................16 H4
Farnaby Close 16 H6
Farriers Gate......................17 C4
Faulkner Road 33 B2
Fedw Wood........................31 C2
Feering Street 21 B1
Fenner Brockway Close 16 G6
Fern Court 32 F5
Fern Rise 13 D4
Fernbank.............................8 E4
Ferncroft Way 3 C5
Ferney Cross......................28 F3
Fernhill 10 G5
Fernleigh Road 28 F4
Fernside 21 B4
Ferry Way 32 F6
Festival Crescent 6 E5
Fetty Place 10 F1
Fforest Glade 16 H2
Ffos y Fran 17 C3
Ffrwd Road 3 A3
Fieldings (7) 8 F5
Fields Avenue 9 B1
Fields Park Avenue............33 A1
Fields Park Court*,
     Fields Park Road 33 B1
Fields Park Crescent.........33 B1
Fields Park Gardens 19 A2
Fields Park Lane................19 A2
Fields Park Road 33 B1
Fields Road (Newport)..33 A2/B1
Fields Road (Pontypool)
....10 F2/G2
Fields View Road 9 B3
Fieldside Court (22) 3 D3
Fifth Street 22 F3
Filey Road 14 F6
Finchway Court (8) 2 F2
Fir Tree Close 16 E1
Fir Tree Cottages 27 C4
Firbank Avenue 16 G2
Firbank Crescent 16 G3
Firs Road 28 E4
Firs, The (Abersychan) 2 H3

Firs, The (Blaenavon) 1 C5
Firs, The (Little Mill) 6 H5
Firs, The (Newport)............13 D5
First Street 22 E3/E4
Firtree Cottages 4 H6
Fisher Close 23 B1
Fishermans Walk 32 F5
Fitzosborn Close................31 D3
Fitzwalter Road..................28 G4
Five Houses (Garndiffaith) ..2 G1
Five Houses (Pontypool) 4 H4
Five Lanes Cottages.........25 C6
Five Locks Close..................7 A6
Five Locks Road.......7 A6/9 A1
Five Oaks Lane....................9 B3
Flats, The 31 D6
Fleetwood Close 21 B2
Fleming Close....................13 D3
Flint Close..........................16 G3
Flint Court 15 C2
Florence Place 6 F2
Foley House (6) 9 C4
Folly Lane 3 D5/D6
Folly Road............................3 D5
Folly View (Pontnewynydd) 3 D2
Folly View (Pontypool) 4 E6/5 A1
Folly View (Upper Race).....4 H4
Ford Farm Lane 24 H2
Ford Street 33 B3
Fordwich Close 31 B1
Forest Close (Cwmbran) 8 G4
Forest Close (Newport)......16 H2
Forest View..........................8 G2
Forge Close 15 C4
Forge Cottages 15 C4
Forge Gardens 31 B1
Forge Hammer Flats*,
     Burford Street 1 B4
Forge Lane (Newport)........17 C5
Forge Lane*, George St......4 F5
Forge Mews 17 C5
Forge Road (Blaenavon) 1 C2
Forge Road (Newport).......17 D5
Forge Row (Caldicot) 29 D1
Forge Row (Pontypool)......4 E3
Forgeside 9 C1
Forgeside Road 1 C3
Forgeside*, Taliesin 9 C1
Fort Lea*, Gaer Road ..19 C2/C3
Fort View............................17 C3
Fosse Close 21 C5
Fosse Lane 16 E4
Fosse Road 21 C5
Foundry Cottages 6 F2
Foundry Road 3 B2
Fountain Cottages (1) 31 B1
Fountain Road 5 C2
Fountain Way 32 G5
Four Ash Court 30 G5
Four Ash Street 30 G5
Four Houses 8 F2
Fourteen Locks Cottages ..12 H5
Fourth Street 22 F3
Fowler Street 4 E4
Foxwood Close 17 C3

Foxwood Court*, Foxwood Close 17 C3
Francis Close 33 D5
Francis Drive.....................19 C5
Francis Morris Estate 1 C5
Francis Street 33 D5
Frank Street 14 H5
Fred Edwards Close 23 D1
Frederick Mews 19 C6
Frederick Street 19 C6
Freeholdland Road 3 C3
Freshwater Road 21 D5
Friars Court......................33 D3
Friars Crescent 33 D3
Friars Field 19 B4
Friars Garden 10 F4
Friars Road......................33 D2
Friars Street 33 B4
Frobisher Road 21 B3
Frome Walk 11 D6
Frondeg...........................5 B5
Fryth Wood 31 C1
Fulford Cottages*, Victoria Av.
......................................16 H1
Fuschia Way.....................12 G1

G

Gables, The*, Bridge St....31 B4
Gaer Lane.......................19 C4
Gaer Park Avenue 19 C1
Gaer Park Drive 19 C1
Gaer Park Hill 19 C1
Gaer Park Lane 19 C1
Gaer Park Parade............19 C1
Gaer Park Road 19 C1
Gaer Road..................19 C2/C3
Gaer Street 19 C3
Gaer Vale 19 D2
Gainsborough Close.........10 G3
Gainsborough Drive..........16 F2
Garage Cottages.............31 A1
Garden City Way 31 C4
Gardens, The 27 B3
Garn Road 1 A1
Garn yr Erw......................1 A1
Garndyrus Mount 1 A4
Garth Close (Newport) 17 C3
Garth Close (Pontypool) 3 C4
Garth Hill 17 C3
Garth Road 8 F6
Garth Terrace 17 C3
Garthalan Drive...............28 H3
Garvey Close 32 G5
Garw Row 9 B4
Garw Wood Drive 9 B3
Garw, The 9 B4
Gaskell Street 21 B2
Gatlas Road 15 A4
Gaudi Walk 12 H3
Gaynors (8) 8 F4
Gelli Fawr Court 8 G3
Gelli Place.........................3 A2
Gelli Rhwy Road.................2 G2
General Rees Square..........9 D1
George Lansbury Drive 16 G6

George Lansbury Home 9 B4
George Street (Blaenavon)..1 C4
George Street (Cwmbran) ..9 C1
George Street (Newport) ..33 D5
George Street (Pontnewynydd)
......................................3 D3
George Street (Pontypool)
......................................4 E4/F5
George Street Flats*, George St.
......................................3 D3
Gerbera Drive 12 G1
Gething Terrace 1 C2
Gibbons Close 21 B5
Gibbs Road 21 A3
Gibraltar Way 32 F6
Gibson Lane 4 F5
Gifford Close 8 F6/10 F1
Gilbert Close 21 A6
Gilchrist Thomas Court 1 B3
Gilchrist Walk 1 B4
Giles Road 1 C5
Gileston Walk 8 E6
Gilwern Farm Close 15 A6
Gilwern Place 7 B6
Glade Close 8 G4
Gladstone Place 6 G2
Gladstone Terrace (Blaenavon)
......................................1 C4
Gladstone Terrace (Varteg) 2 F2
Gladstone Terrace*,
       Osborne Road.............4 E4
Glan Rhyd..........................8 G4
Glan y Nant (Cwmbran) 8 F6
Glan y Nant (Llangybi) 24 F2
Glan y Nant Close...............8 F6
Glan yr Afon 2 H1
Glanmor Court*, Glanmor Cres.
......................................16 H4
Glanmor Crescent.............16 H4
Glanmor Park Avenue 16 H4
Glannant*, Cwmynyscoy Road
......................................4 H6
Glansychan Houses 3 A2
Glansychan Lane 3 A2
Glantorvaen Houses 1 C3
Glantorvaen Road...............4 F5
Glanwern Avenue 16 H5
Glanwern Close 16 H5
Glanwern Drive 16 H5
Glanwern Grove 16 H5
Glanwern House (Newport)16 H5
Glanwern House*, Albion Road
......................................4 G4
Glanwern Rise 16 H5
Glanwern Terrace 4 G4
Glanyravon Cottages*, Isca Rd.
......................................16 E5
Glascoed Road...................5 D5
Glasllwch Crescent 17 A5
Glasllwch Lane 17 C6
Glasllwch View 17 C6
Glaslyn Court 9 B3
Glassworks Cottages 14 F5
Glastonbury Close (2)........14 H5
Glebe Street 21 A1

Glen Court*, Monnow Way 13 D1
Glen Usk View 15 B3
Glen View (Chepstow) 32 G1
Glen View (Cwmbran).........7 D6
Glen View (Garndiffaith) 2 H2
Glen, The*, Old Chepstow Road
......................................23 A5
Glencourt 6 G2
Glengariff Court..................6 F1
Glenside 7 B6
Glenview Road 3 C4
Gloster Place 14 H6
Gloster Street 14 H6
Glosters Parade 6 E5
Gloucester Close 9 D4
Gloucester Court...............15 C3
Gloucester Road 31 A5
Glycoed Way....................28 E5
Glyn View 4 G2
Glyndwr Road 9 D2
Glyntirion 8 F6
Godfrey Road (Cwmbran)....9 B1
Godfrey Road (Newport)....33 A2
Gold Tops 33 A2
Goldcliff Court 10 E2
Goldcliff House*, Goldcliff Court
......................................10 E2
Goldcroft Common 15 D4
Goldcroft Court (2) 15 D4
Goldfinch Close 28 G4
Goldsmith Close 19 D2
Golf Course Lane 12 G3
Golf Road 5 D4
Golynos Place....................2 H1
Golynos Road.....................2 G1
Golynos*, Castlewood 2 H1
Goodrich Court (3) 10 E4
Goodrich Crescent 14 G4
Goodrich Grove 20 H1
Goodrich Lane 14 G4
Goossens Close 23 C2
Gordings 7 D4
Gordon Road 3 A2
Gordon Street 21 A1
Gore Street 14 G6
Govilon Place 7 B6
Gower Green 9 B3
Goya Close 16 G3
Grafton Lane 33 A5
Grafton Road 33 A5
Graham Bell Close 13 C2
Graham Street 33 C3
Grahamstown Grove..........31 C6
Grahamstown Road 31 C6
Graig Close 17 B3
Graig Park Avenue 14 E4
Graig Park Circle...............14 E3
Graig Park Hill 14 E4
Graig Park Lane 14 E4
Graig Park Parade 14 E4
Graig Park Road 14 E4
Graig Park Villas 14 E4
Graig Road 7 B4/D3
Graig View 7 B4
Graig View Terrace.............2 H1

Graig Wood Close..............14 E4
Graigddu View 2 G1
Granary Mews...................23 B4
Grange Cottages...............16 E5
Grange Court (27) (Pontypool)
......................................3 D4
Grange Court (Newport) 33 C1
Grange Lane......................9 C1
Grange Park 31 A1
Grange Path 10 F4
Grange Road (Cwmbran)
......................................9 C2/10 E2
Grange Road (St. Arvans) 31 B1
Grange Road (Undy)..........27 B4
Granston Houses*, Granston Sq.
......................................8 E5
Granston Square................8 E5
Granville Close 17 A5
Granville Lane...................33 C6
Granville Square 33 C6
Granville Street 33 C5
Granville Terrace 31 B5
Grasmere Way 32 G5
Great Oaks Park...............12 G3
Green Acre 10 F1
Green Avenue 28 F4
Green Close 28 G1
Green Cottages...................1 A2
Green Court (Caldicot) 28 G4
Green Court (Cwmbran) 9 B3
Green Farm Cottages 28 E1
Green Fields 2 G2
Green Lane.......................28 G4
Green Meadow 3 A1
Green Moor Lane 27 C2
Green Street (Chepstow) ...31 D4
Green Street (Redwick) 27 D1
Green Way 2 H1
Green, The 4 F3
Greene Close 23 D2
Greenfield (Caerleon) 15 C2
Greenfield (Caldicot) 28 F5
Greenfield Close 7 A6
Greenfield Cottages (5) 2 G1
Greenfield Place 1 C4
Greenfield Road 17 A5
Greenfield Terrace 2 F1
Greenfields View................24 H5
Greenforge Way 7 D5/D6
Greenhill 9 C1
Greenhill Close 6 G2
Greenhill Cottages 9 C1
Greenhill Road 6 G2
Greenhill Road (Cwmbran) ..9 C1
Greenhill Road (Pontypool)..6 F2
Greenland Cottages 3 D1
Greenlands 3 C1
Greenlands Road 3 D4
Greenmeadow Avenue 21 B5
Greenmeadow Close
       (Cwmbran)..................8 E6
Greenmeadow Close
       (Parc-Seymour) 24 E6
Greenmeadow Cottages
       (Cwmbran)..................7 D5

Greenmeadow Cottages
(Caerleon) 15 B3
Greenmeadow Crescent.....6 H6
Greenmeadow Drive 24 F6
Greenmeadow House 8 E6
Greenmeadow Road..........21 B4
Greenmeadow Square 8 E6
Greenmeadow Way 7 D5
Greenway Close 6 F1
Greenway Drive 6 F1
Greenway Walk 6 F1
Greenways, The 27 C3
Greenwich Road...............19 D4
Greenwillows 10 G2
Greenwood Avenue 7 B5
Greenwood Drive 8 G2
Greenwood Flats*, Beaufort Rd.
...............................16 F2
Greenwood Road 2 H2
Grenadier Drive.................23 A4
Grenville Terrace 28 G2
Grey Waters 9 D3
Greys Road.......................4 H5
Griffin Avenue 1 C4
Griffin Court*, Osborne Rd...4 E5
Griffin Street 33 B4
Griffin, The 17 C4
Griffiths Court 1 C2
Griffiths Way.....................2 H2
Grindle Walk 12 H3
Groes Close 12 G4
Groes Road 12 G3/G4
Groes Road 12 H3
Grosmont Place 9 A3
Grosmont Road 5 D5
Grosmont Way 20 H1
Grosvenor Place 6 G2
Grosvenor Road 17 B2
Grove Close 3 D3
Grove Court*, East Grove Road
................................21 A4
Grove Crescent...................3 C4
Grove Estate.....................3 D3
Grove Estate Road 3 D3
Grove Gardens 28 F5
Grove Park 9 A1
Grove Park Avenue.............9 A1
Grove Park Drive 14 E5
Grove Park Roundabout ...14 E5
Grove Place (Cwmbran) 9 A1
Grove Place (Pontypool) 6 F2
Grove Road 3 D3
Grove Terrace (5) 3 D3
Grove, The 33 D4
Grove, The*, Church Rd. ..28 E5
Groves Road....................17 B6
Groveside Villas 3 D3
Gwaenfelin Walk................1 B4
Gwent Square 9 D2
Gwent Street 4 F4
Gwentlands Close.............31 D3
Gwentlands Flats 31 D3
Gwladys Place 15 C3
Gwy Court 31 B4
Gwyn Crescent 2 F2

Gwyndy Road 27 B5
Gwynllyw 7 B5
Gypsy Lane.......................3 D1

H

Haden Street.....................4 F4
Hadrian Close 15 C3
Hafod Close.................15 A2/B6
Hafod Court 33 D1
Hafod Court Road.............33 D1
Hafod Gardens 15 A2/B6
Hafod Mews................15 A2/B6
Hafod Road 15 A2/B6
Hafren Road 7 C4
Haisbro Avenue................16 F1
Haldane Place 13 D3
Haldens, The (24) 8 F4
Half Pennies Estate 15 A6
Halle Close 23 C2
Halstead Street 21 A1
Hamilton Street 21 B2
Hammond Drive 21 B2
Hampden Court.................21 B3
Hampden Road.................21 B3
Hampshire Avenue 21 C4
Hampshire Close 21 C4
Hampshire Crescent 21 C4
Hampton Place 4 E5
Hanbury Close (Caerleon) 16 E5
Hanbury Close (Cwmbran) ..9 C1
Hanbury Gardens 3 D3
Hanbury Road (Pontnewynydd)
................................4 E2
Hanbury Road (Pontypool) ..4 F5
Ham Farm Road..................4 F5
Handel Close 23 C2
Handsworth Street 21 B2
Hanfield Park 9 C3
Hanley Path 8 E6
Hanover Close 31 B2
Hanover Court 31 C5
Harding Avenue 13 C3
Hardwick Avenue 31 D4
Hardwick Hill 31 D3
Hardwick Hill Lane 31 D3
Hardwick Terrace 31 C3
Hardy Close 19 D2
Hardy Court (26) 3 D4
Hargreaves Drive 13 C3
Harlech Close 9 A3
Harlech Drive 17 B2
Harlequin Court 14 G4
Harlequin Drive 14 H4
Harlequin Roundabout 14 G4
Harold Street....................9 B1
Harold Walk (4) 17 A4
Harpers Road 2 H2
Harrhy Street....................33 B3
Harris Home*, Powells Place
................................33 C5
Harrogate Road................16 F1
Harrow Close 15 C2
Harrow Road....................33 A6
Hart Gardens*, Alma St. ..19 C5
Hartridge Farm Road 23 D1

Harvey Close 13 D3
Harwood House*, Ty Box Road
................................9 C1
Hassocks Lea (9) 8 F5
Hathaway Street 21 B2
Hatherleigh 16 H4
Havelock Street 33 C4
Haven, The 5 B5
Hawarden Green (4) 10 E4
Hawarden Road 21 A3
Hawke Close 23 B1
Hawkes Ridge 8 F2
Hawkins Crescent 23 B1
Hawksmoor Close 12 H4
Hawksworth Grove 21 B4
Hawthorn Close (Chepstow)
................................32 F4
Hawthorn Close (Underwood)
................................23 D5
Hawthorn Court.................9 C3
Hawthorn Road..................6 G1
Hawthorne Avenue 21 A3
Hawthorne Close (Undy)....27 B4
Hawthorne Fosse 21 A4
Hawthorne Square 21 A3
Hawthorns, The (Caerleon)15 C4
Hawthorns, The (Cwmbran) 7 B5
Hayling Close 16 G2
Haynes Court*, James St. 19 C6
Hayswayn (10) 8 F4
Hazel Avenue 28 F4
Hazel Close 5 D5
Hazel Road 23 D6
Hazel Walk (Caerleon) 15 D2
Hazel Walk (Cwmbran) 9 B3
Hazell Drive 18 G4
Hazelton Villas 31 D1
Hazlitt Close 19 D2
Headland, The 32 G5
Helford Square 11 D6
Helpstone Terrace.............4 F3
Hendre Court 8 G3
Hendre Farm Court 23 B1
Hendre Farm Drive
................21 A6/23 B1/D1
Hendre Farm Gardens 23 D1
Hendrew Lane..................24 F5
Hendrick Drive 31 C5
Henllys Lane (Cwmbran)
................................8 G2/H3
Henllys Lane (Newport)
...................11 B1/12 E4
Henllys Way 8 G3/G5/10 F1
Henry Morgan Close.........20 G2
Henry Wood Close 21 A5
Henry Wood Walk.............21 A5
Hensol Close (Cwmbran) ..10 E3
Hensol Close (Rogerstone)12 G4

Henson Street....................21 B2
Heol Beuno 5 C3
Heol Deiniol 5 C3
Heol Derwen 5 D4
Heol Glaslyn 28 E6
Heol Isaf 5 D4
Heol Madoc......................5 D4
Heol Newydd....................7 B5
Heol Padarn 5 D4
Heol Pont y Cwcw 20 G3
Heol Teifi 28 E6
Heol Teilo 5 D4
Heol Towy 28 E6
Heol Waun 2 H1
Heol y Pwca 7 B5
Herbert Close 30 H3
Herbert Place 1 C3
Herbert Road 28 E4
Herbert Street 33 D4
Herbert Walk 33 D4
Herberts Close 2 G1
Herberts Road 2 G1
Hereford Court 15 C3
Hereford Street 33 A6
Heron Road 28 G6
Heron Way 20 F3
Heronston Close 27 C6
Hertford Place..................16 G2
Heston Close 29 B4
Hexagon House 18 F5
High Bank 16 F1
High Beech Lane..........31 D2/D3
High Close 10 F4
High Cross Close 17 B5
High Cross Drive 17 A5
High Cross Lane 17 A5/B5
High Cross Road..............17 A5
High Meadow 1 D2
High Street (Abersychan) ...3 A1
High Street (Blaenavon) 1 C3
High Street (Caerleon) 15 D4
High Street (Chepstow) 31 C4
High Street (Garndiffaith) ...2 G1
High Street (Griffithstown)...6 E2
High Street (Newport)......33 A4
High Street (Pontypool) ..4 F4/F5
High View 31 C3
Highcroft Road 14 H3
Highfield (Caerwent)........26 H3
Highfield (Penperlleni)........5 A5
Highfield Close 10 G4
Highfield Close (Caerleon) 15 C2
Highfield Close (Pontypool) 3 D2
Highfield Court 17 C3
Highfield Gardens 17 C3
Highfield Lane.................17 C3
Highfield Road (Bassaleg) 17 C4
Highfield Road (Caerleon) 15 C2
Highfield Road (Newport) ..19 C2
Highfield Way 15 C2
Highland Grove 9 A1
Highmoor Hill 28 E2
Highway, The (Croesyceiliog)
................................9 B4/C4
Highway, The (Cwmbran)..10 G2

Highway, The (Pontypool)
................5 C2/D3/6 E4
Hill Barn View 29 B4/C3
Hill Brow 32 E1
Hill Crest*, High Street 4 F5
Hill Grove 4 E4
Hill Street (Blaenavon) 1 C4
Hill Street (Cwmbran) 10 F1
Hill Street (Griffithstown) 6 E2
Hill Street (Newport) 33 C4
Hill Street (Pontypool)........3 D3
Hill Top 10 E1
Hill View Crescent............21 C4
Hilla Road 33 B2
Hillcrest 15 C2
Hillcrest (Garndiffaith)........2 G2
Hillcrest (New Inn) 5 D5
Hillcrest Road 5 C3
Hillrise 2 H2
Hillside 31 A1
Hillside Avenue 1 B4
Hillside Cottages (Panteg) ..6 F1
Hillside Cottages (Shirenewton)
................................26 E6
Hillside Court 9 C1
Hillside Crescent...............17 A5
Hillside Drive 4 H5
Hillside Road 6 E1
Hillstone Place 9 B2
Hilltop 31 D2
Hilltop Green 7 B6
Hillview 19 C2
Hinter Path (11).................8 F5
Hitchen Hollow 32 G6
Hobart Close.....................19 B1
Hocker Hill Street 31 C4
Hodges Close...................29 B4
Hodges Terrace 7 D6
Hogarth Close (Cwmbran) 10 G3
Hogarth Close (Newport) ..16 G2
Holbein Road 16 G3
Holland Close 12 G3
Hollies, The.....................30 H3
Hollins Close 31 B4
Holly Close 32 F4
Holly Lane.......................24 H5
Holly Lodge Close 9 B4
Holly Lodge Gardens 9 B4
Holly Lodge Green 9 B4
Holly Lodge Nursing Home ..8 F6
Holly Lodge Road 9 B4
Hollybush Avenue.............14 E3
Hollybush Close (Cwmbran) 8 F6
Hollybush Close (Newport) 14 E3
Hollybush Corner 8 F6
Hollybush Cottages*,
Newport Road 6 H4
Hollybush Road 8 G6
Hollybush Terrace..............3 D3
Hollybush View 8 G6
Hollybush Walk 17 B3
Hollybush Way 8 G6
Hollyhock Close 12 H1
Holmdale..........................8 E4
Holst Close 23 C2

Holyoake Terrace (8) (Pontypool)
................................3 D3
Holyoake Terrace*,
Snatchwood Road 3 B3
Home Farm Close.............15 D2
Home Farm Crescent 15 D2
Home Farm Green 15 D2
Honddu Close 28 E5
Honeysuckle Close 17 B5
Hood Road 23 B1/B2
Hop Garden, The (4)..........32 F5
Hopefield 14 G4
Hopefield Court*, Hopefield
................................14 G4
Hopewell Close.................32 F5
Hopkins Walk 23 D2
Hornbeam Close...............15 D1
Hornbeam Walk 17 C3
Horrocks Close 13 C3
Horseshoe Row 1 D5
Hoskins Street 14 G5
Hospital Road 3 D4
Hove Avenue 16 G3
Howard Close 23 B1
Howe Circle 23 B1
Howells Row 31 C4
Hubert Rise (5) 17 A4
Hubert Road 16 G1
Hughes Crescent 31 D4
Humber Close 14 E1
Humber Road 14 E1
Hunter Close....................12 G4
Hunters Ridge 27 B5
Huntfield Cottages 31 C3
Huntfield Road 31 C2
Huntingdon Close 7 D4
Huxley Green 13 D3
Hydrangea Close 17 B5
Hynam Place 2 H2

I

Ifor Hael Road..................12 H3
Ifton Avenue 28 G2
Ifton Lane 28 G2
Ifton Place 21 B3
Ifton Road 28 G2
Ifton Street 21 B3
Ifton Terrace 28 G2
Imperial House 18 G6
Imperial Way....................18 G6
Incline Road 3 A3
Incline Row 2 E2
Incline View.......................2 H2
Industrial Estate Road........4 E2
Ingles (12) 8 F5
Inner Loop Road 32 E6
Iris Road 12 H1
Isca Close 9 C2
Isca Court 15 D3
Isca Mews 15 D5
Isca Road 16 E5
Itchen Close 11 D6
Itchen Road 13 D1
Itton Road 31 B2
Ivor Gardens 1 C4

Ivor John Walk 15 B3
Ivor Street (Blaenavon).......1 C4
Ivor Street (Newport) 33 C4
Ivy Cottages (Chepstow)....31 B6
Ivy Cottages*, Viaduct Rd. ..2 H2
Ivy Dene Close 3 C4
Ivy Road 33 C1

J

Jackson Court....................16 H1
Jackson Place 16 H1
James Street (Newport) 19 C6
James Street (Pontypool)
................................4 E6/5 A1
Jane Austen Close 19 D2
Jane Close 20 G2
Japonica Close 13 C4
Jasmin Close 12 G1
Jasmin Cottages 29 B4
Jeans Close 13 C3
Jeddo Close 19 D5
Jeddo Street 19 C5
Jeffrey Street.....................21 A1
Jellicoe Close 23 B1
Jenkins Street 21 B2
Jerusalem Close 6 E5
Jerusalem Lane 6 E5
Jervis Walk 23 B1
Jessop Close 12 H4
Jessop Road.....................12 H4
Jewell Lane 14 F4
Jim Crow Square 9 C4
John Baker Close 10 G2
John Bull Close.................16 H6
John Field Walk 21 A6
John Frost Square 33 B4
John Ireland Close 21 A6
John Street (Newport).......33 D5
John Street (Pontypool) 4 G5
Johnston Close.................12 G4
Jolyons Court 28 F6
Jones Street 33 C3
Joyce Close 19 C1
Jubilee Place*, Viaduct Rd. 2 H2
Jubilee Terrace 4 E4
Jubilee Way......................28 F5
Jule Road 8 F5
Julius Close 15 C2
Junction 25 (M4) 16 F1
Junction 25a (M4) 14 F5
Junction 26 (M4) 14 F4
Junction 27 (M4) 17 A6
Junction 28 (M4) 18 E5
Junction Road 14 H6
Juniper Crescent 8 G3

K

Kears Row 2 E2
Keats Close (Cwmbran) 8 E6
Keats Close (Newport) 19 D1
Keats Road.......................28 G3
Keene Avenue 17 B5
Keene Street.....................21 B2
Keer Street 33 C5
Kelly Road 16 G3

Kelvedon Street 21 B1
Kelvin Close 13 D3
Kemys Fawr Close 6 G1
Kemys Street.....................6 F2
Kemys Walk 8 F6
Kendall Square 31 C4
Kenfig Place 10 E3
Kenilworth Place 8 F6
Kenilworth Road 21 A3
Kennard Court 1 C3
Kennard Crescent 1 B3
Kennard Place 1 B3
Kennet Grange 24 F2
Kensington Gardens 16 H2
Kensington Grove 21 A2
Kensington Park 27 C3
Kensington Place 16 H2
Kent Close 12 G3
Kent Court.......................15 C3
Kestrel Close 28 G5
Kestrel Way......................20 F1
Keynsham Avenue 33 D4
Kidwelly Close (Cwmbran) 10 E4
Kidwelly Close (Newport) ..20 H1
Kidwelly Road 10 E4
Kier Hardie Crescent 16 G6
Kier Hardie Drive 16 G6
Kiln Way 27 B5
Kimberley Terrace 14 F4
King Alfreds Road.............31 D6
King Street (Blaenavon) 1 B3
King Street (Newport) 33 C4
King Street (Pontypool)......4 F4
Kingfisher Close 28 G5
Kingfisher Place 20 F1
Kings Hill Court*, Stow Hill 19 B3
Kings Lane 33 D4
Kings Parade 19 C6
Kingsacre 33 B1
Kingsdale Court 33 D2
Kingshill Court...................33 C4
Kingsland Walk 8 E5
Kingslea (13) 8 F5
Kingsmark Lane 31 B2
Kingsmill Lane*, Clyffard Cres.
................................19 A4
Kingsmill Terrace 33 C2
Kingston Road 21 A1
Kingsway 33 A4/C5
Kingsway Centre...............33 C4
Kinnock Court 9 B3
Kipling Hill 19 C1
Kipling Road 28 F3
Kirby Daniel Court.............19 C5
Kirby Lane........................19 C5
Kirrlarch Close..................28 F3
Kitchener Street 4 E2
Kitty Hawk Drive 21 C3
Knight Close*, Francis Dr. 19 C5
Knighton Court 15 D4

L

Laburnam Close (Magor) ...27 B5
Laburnam Close (Rogerstone)
................................12 G1

Laburnam Cottages 31 A1
Laburnam Grove 29 B4
Laburnam Terrace 29 B4
Laburnam Way 32 E3
Laburnham Bush Lane 21 B4
Laburnum Cottages (Caerleon)
.................................15 A5
Laburnum Drive (Cwmbran) 8 G3
Laburnum Drive (Newport) 21 A3
Laburnum Drive (Pontypool)5 D5
Laburnum Gardens...........24 H5
Lady Bench 8 F4
Lady Margaret Court (2) ...32 G4
Ladyhill 30 F6
Ladyhill Close 30 F5
Ladyhill Green 21 A5
Ladyhill Road 21 A5
Ladywell 9 B1
Ladywood 30 F6
Lake Road.........................22 E5
Lake Side Close 10 H3
Lake View 10 H3
Lakeside Drive 18 G5
Lamb Close......................19 D1
Lamb Lane 15 A5
Lambert Close 14 G4
Lambert Street 14 G4
Lambourne Crescent 14 E1
Lambourne House 13 D1
Lambourne Walk...............12 E6
Lambourne Way 13 D1
Lancaster Road..................6 F4
Lancaster Way 31 C2
Lancers Way 20 F3
Landau Close 27 B5
Landing, The 3 B1
Landseer Close 16 G3
Langham House 32 E4
Langland Way...................21 D3
Langley Close 27 B3
Langstone Cottages 23 A3
Langstone Court 8 F5
Langstone Court Road 23 B4
Langstone Lane 23 C4
Langstone Rise 24 G2
Lansdown Terrace*,
   Llanover Road.............1 C5
Lansdowne 6 G2
Lansdowne Road (Caerleon)
.................................15 D4
Lansdowne Road (Newport)
.................................19 C2
Lapwing Avenue...............28 G6
Larch Close.......................5 D5
Larch Court......................13 D4
Larch Grove (Newport) 13 C4/D4
Larch Grove (Underwood) 23 D5
Larkfield Avenue 31 D3
Larkfield Close 15 C2
Larkfield House*, Larkfield Park
.................................31 D3
Larkfield Park 31 D3
Larkhill Close 31 D3
Lasgarn Lane 2 H5/3 A4
Lasgarn Place...................3 B3

Lasgarn View (Garndiffaith) 2 H2
Lasgarn View (Varteg) 2 F2
Lasgarn View*, Bluetts Rd...2 H2
Lasgarn Villas 3 A3
Latch Square*, Alma St. 19 C5
Laurel Close 27 B5
Laurel Crescent (Newport) 13 D4
Laurel Crescent (Undy)......27 C5
Laurel Drive (Newport) 17 C4
Laurel Drive (Penperlleni) ...5 A5
Laurel Green 7 B5
Laurel Park 31 B1
Laurel Road 17 B2
Laurel Walk 7 B5
Laurels, The 26 E6
Lavender Way 12 G1
Lavery Close.....................16 G3
Lawns, The (Magor) 27 C3
Lawns, The (Usk) 30 G5
Lawrence Court*,
   Lawrence Hill Avenue 21 A4
Lawrence Crescent...........26 G3
Lawrence Hill 16 H4/21 A3
Lawrence Hill Avenue 21 A3
Laybourne Close................9 C1
Lea Close (Newport) 14 E1
Lea Close (Undy) 27 B4
Leach Road 11 C5
Leadon Court 7 C4
Leas, The.....................7 B5/B6
Ledbrook Close 8 F6
Ledbury Street 14 H5
Lee Way 21 C5/22 E5
Leechpool Holdings 29 A4
Leeway Court 21 D5
Leicester Drive 7 D4
Leicester Road 16 H1
Leigh Road 3 D4
Leighton Court 8 E6
Lennard Street 21 A1
Leslie Green Court 20 E2
Leslie Terrace (6) 17 A4
Lethbridge Terrace 3 B2
Lewis Close (Garndiffaith) ..2 G1
Lewis Close (Newport) 19 C5
Lewis Street 3 A2
Lewis Terrace 3 D4
Lewis View (7)..................17 A4
Lewis Way 32 G5
Lewis Wood 3 D2
Leybourne Houses 30 G5
Libeneth Road 21 B3
Lighthouse Park Estate......20 F2
Lighthouse Road...............20 E2
Lilac Grove 12 G1
Lilburne Drive 21 B2
Lilleshall Street 21 B1
Lily Way 12 G1
Lime Close 19 D5
Lime Crescent 21 B4
Lime Grove 23 A5
Limekiln Road 3 C3
Limes, The 27 B4
Lincoln Close 16 H2
Lincoln Court....................15 C3

Lindbergh Close 21 C3
Linden Close 32 F3
Linden Court 8 F5
Linden Road 21 A3
Link Road 5 D4
Links, The 3 C5
Linley Close 23 C2
Linnet Road 28 G5
Linton Court 3 B3
Linton Street 19 C6
Lion Court 1 B4
Lion Street.........................1 B4
Liscombe Street 21 B2
Lister Green 13 D3
Liswerry Close (5) 10 E4
Liswerry Drive...........9 D4/10 E4
Liswerry Park Drive...........21 B5
Liswerry Road 21 A5/B4/B5
Little Innage Barns 32 H2
Little Oaks View 12 G3
Littledene 8 E4
Livale Close 13 D2
Livale Court......................13 D1
Livale Road 13 D2
Livale Walk 13 D1
Liverpool Street................16 H1
Livingstone Place 21 A1
Llan Honddu 3 B3
Llanarth Street 33 B4
Llandaff Green 9 C2
Llandaff Street 33 D2
Llandegfedd Close 12 G4
Llandegfedd Way 6 E4
Llandegveth Close 9 B4
Llandenny Walk 10 E2
Llanderfel Court 7 C4
Llandowlais Street.............10 F1
Llanerch Close 4 E4
Llanerch Path 8 E5
Llanfoist Crescent 1 B4/B5
Llanfrechfa Way 10 E2
Llangattock Court 9 B4
Llangorse Drive 12 G4
Llangorse Path 10 F3
Llangorse Road................10 E3
Llanon House 9 A2
Llanover Close (Newport) ..14 E3
Llanover Close*, Llanover Road
.................................1 C5
Llanover Road (Blaenavon) 1 C4
Llanover Road (Varteg).......2 E3
Llanover Road Estate 1 C5
Llantarnam Bypass..10 H4/13 B4
Llantarnam Close 10 F2
Llantarnam Gardens.........10 H4
Llantarnam House 10 H2
Llantarnam Park Way 10 H2
Llantarnam Road 10 E2/F2
Llanthewy Close 9 B4
Llanthewy Road 33 C1
Llanthony Close 28 F6
Llanvair Road (Caerwent) ..26 F2
Llanvair Road (Newport)....14 H6
Llanwern Road (Magor) 27 C1
Llanwern Road (Newport)..23 B1

Llanwern Street.................21 A1
Llanyravon Square 10 E3
Llanyravon Way 10 E3
Llew a Dor Court*, Broadwell Ct.
.................................15 D4
Llewellin Street 21 A3
Llewellyn Grove 13 C3
Llewellyn House 10 E2
Llewellyn Walk 13 C3
Lloyd Street......................21 B3
Llwyn Celyn.......................8 F6
Llwyn Deri Close 17 C2
Llwyn Deri Road 33 B1
Llwyn On (Ponthir).......15 A3/B6
Llwyn Onn (Cwmbran) 9 C4
Llwyn y Llan Flats 3 D5
Llyn Berwyn Close 12 G4
Llyn Celyn Close...............12 G4
Llys Gaer*, Stow Park Crescent
.................................19 B3
Llys Gwyrdd 8 G3
Llys Tadcu*, Maryport St. ..30 G5
Llyswen Walk 10 F3
Llywelyn Road 9 D1
Lock Up Lane 3 B2
Locke Street 33 A3
Lodden Close 14 E1
Lodge Avenue 15 C3
Lodge Hill (Caerleon) 15 C2
Lodge Hill (Llanwern) 23 C4
Lodge Road (Caerleon) 15 D3
Lodge Road (Talywain).......3 A1
Lodge Way 29 C1
Lodges, The*, Wednesbury St.
.................................21 B2
Lodgewood 5 C2
Lon Helyg 9 C4
Lon Nant 9 B2
London Street 16 H1
Long Acre (14) 8 F5
Long Hollow 9 C1
Long Row 4 H4
Longbridge 15 A1/B5
Longcroft Road.................28 G4
Longditch Road................21 D6
Longfellow Close 28 G3
Longfellow Court...............28 G3
Longfellow Place 28 G3
Longfellow Road...............28 G3
Longhouse Barn 5 A5
Longhouse Grove 8 G3
Longmeadow Court...........21 B5
Longtown Grove 20 H1
Lookout Cottages*, Mounton Rd.
.................................31 C2
Loop Road 32 E6
Lord Eldon Drive 32 G4
Lord Street 14 H6
Loreto House*, Allt yr Yn Avenue
.................................4 H3
Lower Bridge Street 4 F5
Lower Church Street..........31 B4
Lower Dock Street 33 C5
Lower Ellick Street*, Ellick Street
.................................1 B4

Lower Garn Terrace 1 A2
Lower Glantorvaen Terrace 1 C3
Lower Harpers Road...........2 H3
Lower Hill Street (7) 1 C4
Lower Leigh Road.............3 C3
Lower Market Arcade*, Crane St.
...........................4 F5
Lower Park Gardens...........4 E5
Lower Park Terrace 4 G5
Lower Pentwyn Cottages ..30 H3
Lower Stoney Road 2 H2
Lower Ty Gwyn Road........2 G2
Lower Waun Street 1 B3
Lower Woodland Street 1 B4
Lowlands Court.................9 B1
Lowlands Crescent 9 A1
Lowlands Road 9 B1
Lowndes Close 17 B3
Lucas Street 14 H4
Ludlow Close (Cwmbran) ..10 F4
Ludlow Close (Newport) 21 B2
Lulworth Road.................16 E5
Lundy Drive 16 G2
Lupin Grove 12 H1
Lyncroft............................7 D4
Lyndhurst Avenue 19 D3
Lyndon Way (8).................17 A4
Lyne Road 14 G5
Lysted House*,
   Greenmeadow Way......8 E6

M

Macarthys Court 33 B4
Macaulay Gardens 19 D2
Machine Meadow 3 D3
Madocke Road 31 D6
Maendy Place 7 B5
Maendy Square...................7 B5
Maendy Way 7 A5/9 C1
Maendy Wood Rise.............7 B5
Maerdy Close 19 D3
Maes y Celyn 5 D1
Maes y Rhiw Court 7 D3
Maesderwen Crescent 5 C1
Maesderwen Rise 5 D1
Maesderwen Road 5 C1
Maesglas Avenue 19 D3
Maesglas Close 20 E3
Maesglas Crescent 20 E2
Maesglas Grove 20 E2
Maesglas Road.................20 E3
Maesglas Street 20 E3
Maesgwyn.........................7 A6
Magna Porta Gardens 10 H4
Magnolia Close (Chepstow)
...........................32 F5
Magnolia Close (Newport) 13 C4
Magor Court 27 B3
Magor Road 27 A1
Magor Street 21 B2
Main Road (Magor)............27 C4
Main Road (Portskewett) ..29 C3
Maindee Parade 16 H1
Maindee Terrace.................7 B6
Major Close.......................8 E3

Malcolm Sargent Close......21 B6
Mall, The.............................9 D2
Mallard Avenue.................28 G5
Mallard Way 20 G2
Mallards Reach..................30 G2
Malmesbury Close (3)........14 H5
Malpas Court 13 C2
Malpas Court Estate 13 D3
Malpas Lane 14 F4
Malpas Road......13 C3/14 E3/F4
Malpas Street 10 E1
Malthouse Lane (Caerleon)
...........................15 A1/B5
Malthouse Lane (Pontypool) 4 E4
Malthouse Road ....13 A
Malvern Close (Newport) ..16 F2
Malvern Close (Risca)........12 E1
Malvern Road 33 B6
Manchester Street ..16 H1/33 A6
Manley Road.....................33 C1
Manor Chase 27 C5
Manor Court (Rogiet) 28 G2
Manor Court (Usk) 30 H6
Manor Gate.......................7 D5
Manor Park 20 G2
Manor Road 2 H2/3 A1/A2
Manor View 31 B1
Manor Way (Abersychan) 3 A2
Manor Way (Chepstow) 31 C3
Manor Way (Portskewett) ..29 C2
Manor Wood 31 C1
Manorbier Drive 10 E3
Mansel Street 21 A3
Maple Avenue 32 E3/F4
Maple Close (Caldicot) 28 F4
Maple Close (Underwood) 23 D5
Maple Crescent 6 G1
Maple Road.........................6 F1
Maple Road South 6 G1
Marconi Close...................13 D2
Margaret Avenue 14 G6
Margretts Way..................28 F5
Marigold Close 12 G1
Marina Court 16 F1
Marine Terrace 29 C3
Mariner Way 22 E1
Mariners Reach 32 G5
Marion Place....................19 D5
Marion Street 19 D5
Market Arcade*, Crane St. ..4 F5
Market Arcade*, High St. ..19 A5
Market Street (Blaenavon) ..1 C4
Market Street (Newport) ...33 D6
Market Street (Pontypool) 4 F5
Market Street Court*, Market St.
...........................4 F5
Market Street Square*,
   Market Street..............4 F5
Marl Court 7 C4
Marlborough Road (Cwmbran)
...........................7 D3
Marlborough Road (Newport)
...........................33 A6
Marloes Path.....................7 D4
Marlowe Close 12 H4

Marlowe Gardens 19 D2
Marryat Walk....................19 D2
Marsh Road 32 E4
Marshfield Road 30 E1
Marshfield Street...............21 C2
Marston Court...................14 G4
Marston Path.....................8 E5
Marten Road 32 E4
Martin Close 28 G1
Martin Terrace 1 C2
Martindale Road 6 F2
Martins Road 26 H3
Martins Row 27 C4
Martins, The.....................31 B5
Mary Street (6) 1 C4
Maryport Street.................30 G5
Marysfield Close 30 H3
Masefield Road.................28 G4
Masefield Vale 19 C2
Masie Court 19 C5
Mathern Road 32 G2/E3
Mathern Way....................32 E4
Matthew Terrace..................3 D3
Maugham Close 19 D2
Maxworthy Row 1 B4
May Cottages 17 A3
May Street.......................21 A1
Maybury House*, Byways....8 E5
Maynes (15) 8 F4
McIntyre Court*, Commercial St.
...........................6 E2
Mead Lane (Cwmbran)........9 C1
Mead Lane (Redwick)........27 D1
Meadow Bank 5 A5
Meadow Brook Avenue........7 A6
Meadow Close 6 G2
Meadow Croft 28 G1
Meadow Lane (Chepstow) 31 C3
Meadow Lane (Cwmbran) ..9 C4
Meadow Rise 27 B4
Meadow Walk 31 C3
Meadow Way 5 A5
Meadowland Drive 12 G1
Meadowlands Close 24 F6
Meadows Road 22 F5
Meadows, The (Magor)......27 C3
Meadows, The (Marshfield)
...........................30 G2
Meadows, The (Usk) 30 G6
Meads Close 21 C4
Meads Court 32 E4
Meadway 28 G1
Medlock Close 13 D1
Medlock Crescent 13 D1
Medlock Walk 13 D1
Medway Close 11 D6
Medway Court..................11 D6
Medway Road...................11 D5
Melbourne Court 8 E6
Melbourne Way 17 C6/19 B1
Melfort Gardens 19 C2
Melfort Road 19 B2
Melling Court*, Osborne Road
...........................4 F5
Mellon Street....................33 C5

Melyn Bach Avenue 6 G6
Mendalgief Road...............19 C5
Mendip Close 16 H5
Meon Close......................13 D2
Merchants Hill 4 E4
Merchants Hill Close...........4 E4
Mercian Way 31 D6
Mere Path 7 D4
Meredith Close 19 C3
Merlin Close*, Barn Owl Road
...........................28 G1
Merlin Crescent 16 G2
Merriotts Place 16 H1
Merrivale Cottages 27 C3
Mersey Walk 12 E6
Merton Green 26 F2
Mervyn Terrace (Pontnewynydd)
...........................3 D2
Mervyn Terrace (Pontypool) 4 E5
Methuen Road 21 A1
Mews, The (Newport) 19 A3
Mews, The*, Crane Street....4 F5
Meyricks, The.....................8 G4
Michael Way 4 E5
Middle Coed Cae 1 C5
Middle Street....................31 C4
Middle Way 32 F4
Midfield 5 B5
Milford House*, Farlow Wk. 8 E6
Mill Common....................27 C4
Mill Heath 13 D1
Mill Heath Home*, Parret Road
...........................13 D2
Mill Lane (Caldicot)...........28 G5
Mill Lane (Castleton).........30 E1
Mill Lane (Chepstow) 31 C4
Mill Lane (Cwmbran) 8 G4
Mill Parade 19 D6
Mill Reen........................27 B4
Mill Road..........................3 D4
Mill Street (Caerleon) 15 D4
Mill Street (Newport) 33 A4
Mill Street (Usk) 30 H5
Millbrook Court (Little Mill) ..6 H6
Millbrook Court (Undy) 27 C4
Millbrook Lane..................25 A3
Millbrook Place 6 H6
Miller Close 24 H2
Millers Ride 10 E3
Millfield Park 27 B4
Milman Street 19 D5
Milner Street 21 B2
Milton Close 8 E6
Milton Court.....................23 B1
Milton Hill 23 C3
Milton Road......................21 A2
Minories (16) 8 F5
Miskin Court 27 C6
Miskin Green......................9 D3
Miskin House*, Miskin Grn...9 D3
Mission Hall Road...............3 B1
Mitchell Close 10 F5
Mitchell Terrace (2).............3 D3
Mithras Way 15 C3

Mobile Homes*, Brynwern....**4** F4
Model Cottages (Chepstow)
..................................**32** G1
Model Cottgaes (Sedbury) **31** D6
Mole Close **11** D6
Molescombe (17) **8** F5
Mon Cottages*, Kemys St. ..**6** F2
Mona Close.......................**9** C2
Mona Cottages **30** G5
Monet Crescent **16** G3
Monks Close.....................**28** F5
Monmouth Close................**6** E4
Monmouth Court...............**33** D1
Monmouth Crescent **6** F4
Monmouth Drive **16** F3
Monmouth House*,
Allt yr Yn View **14** H2
Monmouth House*,
Monmouth Square........**9** D2
Monmouth Road (St. Arvans)
...................................**31** B1
Monmouth Road (Usk) **30** G5
Monmouth Square **9** D2
Monmouth Walk*, Monmouth Sq.
..................................**9** D2
Monnow Court **7** C3
Monnow Walk **11** D6
Monnow Way
...........**11** D6/**13** D2/**14** E1
Mons Close.......................**14** H3
Montague Almshouse*,
Upper Church Street ..**31** C4
Montgomery Road **13** C3
Montreal Close **17** B6
Montresor Court **10** H4
Moor Street.......................**31** C3
Moore Crescent **23** C2
Moorings, The (Newport) ..**16** F2
Moorings, The (Pontypool) ..**5** D2
Moorland Avenue **21** B5
Moorland Park...................**21** B5
Moorlands View **28** G6
Mopla Cottages................**31** A5
Mopla Road.......................**31** A4
Morden Lane **16** G1
Morden Road **16** G1
Moreton Street **4** F4
Morgan Rise (2) **1** B4
Morgan Street (Blaenavon)..**1** C4
Morgan Street (Newport) ..**14** G6
Morgan Way **20** G2
Morgraig Avenue.........**20** G1/H1
Morley Drive **21** A6
Morris Rise (3) **1** B4
Morris Street..........**21** A1/**33** C6
Morton Way **19** D2
Moseley Terrace **9** A2
Moss Road **7** D5
Mount Ballan....................**29** A1
Mount Bax........................**21** A5
Mount Pleasant (Chepstow)
..................................**31** D3
Mount Pleasant (Newport) **13** D3
Mount Pleasant (Pontnewynydd)
...................................**3** D3

Mount Pleasant (Talywain) ..**3** A2
Mount Pleasant Close.........**9** B1
Mount Pleasant Court*,
Nicholas Street **4** G5
Mount Pleasant Hill............**9** B1
Mount Pleasant Road ..**7** B6/**9** B1
Mount Road **3** D6
Mount Way **31** B3/C3
Mount, The*, St. Johns Crescent
...................................**4** E3
Mountain Lane **6** E1
Mountain Road (Cwmbran)..**7** A4
Mountain Road (Risca) **12** E1
Mountain View Road...........**3** D3
Mountbatten Close **23** B2
Mountford Close **12** G4
Mountjoy Place **33** D5
Mountjoy Road **33** D5
Mountjoy Street.................**33** D5
Mounton Close **31** D2
Mounton Drive **31** D2
Mounton Road..............**31** C2/D1
Mountside **12** E1
Moxon Road **14** E3
Moyle Grove **15** A2/B6
Mulberry Close **12** G1
Mulcaster Avenue.............**21** C4
Munnings Drive.................**16** G3
Museum Court (Griffithstown)
...................................**6** F2
Museum Court*, Museum Street
..................................**15** D4
Museum Street **15** D4
Mynydd Court **4** H5
Mynydd Maen Road **7** A5
Mynydd View **4** H5
Myra Hess Close...............**23** B2
Myrtle Close **17** B5
Myrtle Cottages **16** E5
Myrtle Drive **17** B5
Myrtle Grove **21** A4
Myrtle Place **31** C4
Myrtles, The **31** B5

N

Nant Celyn Close **7** B5
Nant y Milwr Close **8** G3
Nantcoch Drive **19** A1
Nantymoor Cottages..........**18** G4
Nany y Moor Close............**18** G4
Narberth Crescent.............**10** E4
Narbeth Close...................**20** H1
Narbeth Mews*, Narbeth Close
..................................**20** H1
Nash Close **12** H2
Nash Drive **21** C4
Nash Grove **21** B4
Nash Mead **22** E5
Nash Road **21** C4/D4/**22** F4
Neath Court **7** D4
Neath Villas **3** B2
Neddern Close **28** E5
Neddern Court **28** E4
Neddern Way **28** E4
Neerings **8** F3

Nelson Drive **23** C1
Nelson Street **31** C4
Neston Road.....................**16** H6
Nethercourt (6) **10** E4
Netherwent View...............**27** B3
Neuadda Close..................**17** C2
Nevern Walk (6) **10** E4
Neville Street **2** H2
Neville Terrace **1** A4
New Barn Path **10** F4
New Chapel Court*, Waun Road
...................................**8** F6
New Cottages (Caerwent) **26** G2
New Cottages*, East Usk Road
..................................**14** H5
New Houses (6) (Garndiffaith)
...................................**2** G1
New Houses (Pontypool) **4** G4
New James Street **1** C4
New Market Street **30** G5
New Pastures **19** C3
New Quay Road **22** E1
New Queen Street **1** B4
New Road (Caerleon) **16** E5
New Road (Caldicot) **28** F4
New Road (Garndiffaith).....**2** G1
New Road (Pontypool) **6** E2
New Road (Talywain) **3** A3
New Row............................**8** F2
New Ruperra Street **33** D5
New Street (Cwmbran) **9** B1
New Street (Newport) **19** C6
New Terrace **3** D3
New William Street **1** C4
Newchurch Court **8** E6
Newgale House*, St. Davids Rd.
...................................**9** D2
Newgale Row **10** E2
Newlands Court (12)............**3** D3
Newman Close **23** C1
Newman Road **3** C4
Newnham Place **10** E2
Newport Arcade*, High St. **19** A5
Newport Road (Caldicot)
.........................**28** F3/F5/G4
Newport Road (Castleton) **30** E1
Newport Road (Chepstow)
..........................**31** D2/**32** E1
Newport Road (Cwmbran)
.........................**10** H4/**13** B3
Newport Road (Magor) **27** B3
Newport Road (Pontypool)
...................**6** G4/H4/**9** A4
Newport Road (Pwllmeyric)
..................................**32** E1
Newton Green Cottages ...**32** F1
Newton Manor **26** F5
Newton Way **13** D3
Newton Wynd (18) **8** F5
Newtown Road **5** B5
Neyland Path (19) **8** E5
Nicholas Street **4** G5
Nidd Close **12** E6
Nidd Walk **12** E6
Nightingale Close **28** G5

Nightingale Court **12** E6
Nightingale House **9** C1
Nightingale Terrace **3** D3
Nile Street **10** F1
Nolton Place **8** F5
Nook, The*, Pisgah Road ...**2** H1
Norbury House **8** E6
Norfolk Close **7** D3
Norfolk Road....................**16** H2
Norman Boult Green.........**21** B5
Norman Court **28** G5
Norman Street **15** D4
Norman Terrace **15** D4
Norman Way.....................**29** C1
Normands House **8** F5
Normandy Way **31** B2
Norse Way **31** D6
North Court (20) **3** D3
North Lake Drive...............**18** H6
North Road (Abersychan) ...**3** B3
North Road (Cwmbran) **9** B3
North Road (Pontypool) **4** F4
North Row.........................**27** D1
North Street (Blaenavon) ...**1** B3
North Street (Newport) **33** B4
North View **3** C3
North Walk **9** D2
Northfield Close **15** C2
Northfield Road.................**15** C2
Northumberland Road **16** H2
Novello Walk.....................**23** D1
Nurseries, The **23** A5

O

O'Neal Avenue **22** E3
Oak Bluff **32** E1
Oak Close (Chepstow) **32** F3
Oak Close (Undy)..............**27** B4
Oak Cottages **26** E6
Oak Court (13) **3** D3
Oak Road **12** H2
Oak Street (Cwmbran) **10** E1
Oak Street (Newport)
........................**14** F6/**16** F1
Oak Tree Close...................**5** D4
Oak Tree Court **10** F2
Oak Tree Drive **12** G1
Oak View **1** C5
Oakdale Close **15** D2
Oakdale Path **8** E6
Oakdale Place **3** D3
Oakfield (Caerleon)...........**15** C2
Oakfield Avenue **31** C2
Oakfield Gardens..............**33** B1
Oakfield Road (Cwmbran)..**10** F2
Oakfield Road (Newport) ..**33** B1
Oakfield Terrace **1** C4
Oakfields (Marshfield)........**30** H2
Oakgrove **31** B1
Oaklands **15** A1/B5
Oaklands Park **29** B2
Oaklands Park Drive.........**17** C2
Oaklands Road (Newport) **16** H2
Oaklands Road (Pontypool) **6** G1
Oaklands Terrace **10** G1

Oaklands View 7 D3
Oakleigh Court 8 G2
Oakley Close...................28 F3
Oakley Street 21 B2
Oakley Way....................28 F4
Oaks Close 19 C3
Oaks Court 3 B2
Oaks Court Estate*, Oaks Court
....3 B2
Oaks Road 3 B2
Oaks, The (Cwmbran) 9 C4
Oaks, The (Llangybi).........24 F2
Oaks, The (Underwood) ...23 C5
Oaksford 8 E3
Oat Lane 24 F6
Octagon, The 32 E4
Octavius Close 20 G2
Offas Close 31 D5
Offway 8 G5
Ogmore Crescent 12 E6
Ogmore Place................10 E4
Ogwen House 8 E5
Old Bailey 5 C1
Old Barn Court 27 B6
Old Barn Estate..............16 F2
Old Bridge Road 7 B4
Old Bulwark Road...........31 D3
Old Cardiff Road 20 E2
Old Castle Close.............20 H1
Old Chepstow Road 23 A3/A5
Old Estate Yard*, Fountains Rd.
....5 C2
Old Green Court 30 H3
Old Green Interchange ...33 A4
Old Hall Close................20 F3
Old Hill (Chepstow)...........31 B4
Old Hill (Newport) 16 F5
Old Hill Crescent 16 F5
Old Houses 3 B2
Old James Street 1 C4
Old Lane 3 A2
Old Langstone Court Road
....23 A4
Old Market Street 30 G5
Old Oak Close.................32 F5
Old Paddocks 23 A5
Old Penygarn 4 E5
Old Road...........................3 B3
Old Roman Road 24 G1
Old Row (Cwmbran) 8 F2
Old Row (Sudbrook)........29 D4
Old School Hill 26 E6
Old School Place (10)........3 D2
Old Shirenewton Road 26 G6
Old Stone Road 27 B5
Old William Street.............1 C4
Old Yard Estate 5 C2
Oldbridge Court................7 B4
Oldbury Road 10 E2
Oliphant Circle 13 C2
Oliver Road.......................21 B3
Olway Close..................... 10 F4
Olympia House*, Upper Dock St.
....33 B4
Ombersley Lane 19 B3

Ombersley Road..............33 C1
Open Hearth Close 6 F2
Orangery Walk 20 F2
Orchard Avenue 32 E3
Orchard Close (Caldicot) ..28 G4
Orchard Close (Marshfield)
....30 H2
Orchard Close (Newport) ..17 C2
Orchard Close (Pontypool) ..3 C4
Orchard Court*, Orchard Street
....14 G6
Orchard Farm Close 31 D6
Orchard Farm Estate 3 D5
Orchard Gardens (Chepstow)
....31 B4
Orchard Gardens (Portskewett)
....29 C2
Orchard Lane (Cwmbran)....9 C2
Orchard Lane (Newport)...16 G1
Orchard Mews 14 G6
Orchard Place.................10 E1
Orchard Rise (Chepstow) ..32 F1
Orchard Rise (Shirenewton)
....26 F5
Orchard Road 15 B3
Orchard Street 14 G6
Orchard, The (Caerleon)
...............................15 A2/B6
Orchard, The*, Church Road
....27 C6
Orchid Court 8 F3
Orchid Drive 28 H6
Orchid Meadow 32 F1
Oriel Road........................21 A1
Ormerod Road 31 D6
Osborne Close 16 H1
Osborne Road 4 E4/E5
Osprey Drive...................28 G6
Oswald Road 19 D5
Otter Close 11 D6
Owen Close 15 B3
Owendale Terrace 3 B3
Oxford Close...................15 C2
Oxford Street (Chepstow)..31 C4
Oxford Street (Newport) ...21 A1
Oxford Street (Pontypool) ..6 E2
Oxford Terrace 1 C2
Oxtens 8 G5
Oxwich Grove 18 H6
Oxwich Road 21 D2
Oystermouth Mews...........20 H1
Oystermouth Way.............20 H1

P

Pace Road 8 F4
Padarn Place 9 C1
Paddock Close 7 B6
Paddock Rise 10 F4
Paddock, The (Thornbury) 32 E3
Paddocks, The (Caerleon) 15 C2
Paddocks, The (Cwmbran) 10 F4
Paddocks, The (Undy) 27 B6
Palm Close 5 C5
Palm Square 21 A3
Palmyra Place.................33 C4

Pandy 7 D5
Pant Glas Cottages...........13 A1
Pant Glas Lane*, Pentre Lane
....13 B1
Pant Glas Road................13 A1
Pant Gwyn Close 8 F3
Pant Lane 14 F4
Pant Road 14 F4
Pant yr Eos 9 C1
Pant yr Heol Close 8 G3
Panteg Way 6 E3
Pantglas 3 B1
Pantglas Court 17 C2
Parade, The 9 D2
Parc Avenue 9 B1
Parc Close.......................24 F1
Parc Road 24 F1
Parc y Brain Lane 5 B5
Parc y Brain Road 12 F5
Pardoe Thomas Close*,
Coulson Close...........19 C5
Parfitt Street 21 B4
Parfitt Terrace 7 B6
Park Avenue (Newport) 19 D2
Park Avenue (Rogerstone) 12 H2
Park Close (Cwmbran) 8 G2
Park Close (Newport) 20 E2
Park Cottages (Pontypool) ..5 B1
Park Cottages*, The Park ...1 B3
Park Court (Undy).............27 C6
Park Court*, Park Road 4 E5
Park Crescent (Newport) ..20 E2
Park Crescent (Pontypool)
...............................4 E6/5 A1
Park Drive 19 D2
Park End 23 A5
Park End Court 23 A5
Park Gardens (Blaenavon) ..1 B3
Park Gardens (Newport)...19 D2
Park Gardens (Pontypool) ..4 E5
Park Homes 12 F1
Park House Flats................4 F5
Park Lane*, Park Street 1 C3
Park Road (Caldicot)........28 F4
Park Road (Pontypool) ..4 E5/F5
Park Square 33 C4
Park Street (Blaenavon) 1 C3
Park Street (Pontypool)........6 E2
Park Terrace (3) 3 D3
Park View (Chepstow) 31 B2
Park View (Cwmbran).........9 B2
Park View (Newport).........17 C5
Park View (Pontnewynydd)..3 C3
Park View (Pontypool) 4 G6/5 C1
Park View (Sedbury).........31 C6
Park View Gardens...........17 C5
Park View Terrace 3 C3
Park, The 1 B3
Parkers Row 3 A2
Parkes Lane 4 G3
Parkfield Place 33 B2
Parklands (Mathern).........32 G1
Parklands (Penperlleni).......5 A6
Parklands Close (Cwmbran)
....9 B1

Parklands Close (Newport)
....17 B5
Parklawn Close 9 B1
Parkside (Cwmbran) 10 E1
Parkside (Pontypool)..........4 F5
Parkside Court (28).............3 D4
Parkview 5 B5
Parkwood Close 15 D1
Parkwood Drive 17 C2
Parret Close 13 D2
Parret Road 13 D2
Parret Walk 13 D2
Parry Drive 21 A5
Partridge Way 20 F2
Pastures, The 9 D2
Patti Close.......................23 B2
Pauls End Court 33 C4
Paxton Walk 12 G3
Pear Tree Lane 21 B4
Peartree Close 15 D1
Peartree Cottages.............5 B6
Pembrey Path 7 D6
Pembroke Close 27 B6
Pembroke Court 27 B6
Pembroke Grove..............21 C3
Pembroke Place (Cwmbran)
....10 E4
Pembroke Place (Varteg) ...2 E2
Pembroke Road 32 E3
Pembroke Terrace 2 E2
Pen Bedw 9 C4
Pen Mynydd Close 1 B5
Pen y Bryn 4 E6/5 A1
Pen y Bryn Close 13 D1
Pen y Cae Cottages 30 F2
Pen y Groes Grove..........17 C2
Pen y Lan Road 17 D3/18 F1
Pen y Llan Lane 5 C6
Pen y Parc 9 A1
Penarth Court 10 F4
Pencarn Avenue 18 G6
Pencarn Lane 18 G6/20 G1
Pencarn Way 18 F6/20 G1
Pencoed Place 9 A3
Penda Place 31 D6
Pendine Walk 8 E5
Pendoylan Walk 8 F6
Penhow Mews 20 H1
Penkin Close...................21 A6
Penkin Hill......................21 A6
Penllyn Avenue (Cwmbran) 9 B1
Penllyn Avenue (Newport) 19 B2
Penllyn Lane 19 B2
Penmaes Road..................7 D3
Penney Crescent 13 C2
Pennyfarthing Lane...........27 C4
Pennyfields 7 D5
Penrhos Villas 15 A3
Penrice Green (8) 10 E4
Pensarn Way 8 G3
Pensidan View 17 C2
Penterry Park 31 C2
Pentonville 33 A3
Pentovey Place.................6 H5
Pentre Close....................8 G4

Pentre Lane 11 A4/13 B1
Pentre Tai Lane 12 H1/17 A1
Pentre Tai Road 17 B1
Pentrepoeth Close 17 D2
Pentrepoeth Road.............17 D1
Pentrepoid Road 3 C2/D3
Pentwyn Close 32 E1
Pentwyn Heights.................3 B2
Pentwyn Lane (Abersychan)3 B2
Pentwyn Lane (Newport) ..13 D1
Pentwyn Pitch*, Pentwyn Lane
............................13 D1
Pentwyn Road.............3 B2/C2
Pentwyn Terrace (Abersychan)
............................3 B2
Pentwyn Terrace (Marshfield)
............................30 H3
Pentwyn Villas*, Pentwyn Road
............................3 B2
Penwern Cottages 5 A6
Penycae Road 2 H2
Penygarn Road 3 D5/4 E5
Penygraig Terrace 4 G6
Penygroes Cottages 17 D1
Penylan Close (Newport) ..17 C3
Penylan Close (Pontypool) ..5 D5
Penylan Cottages 18 F1
Penylan Court...................8 G5
Penylan Fields...................2 F2
Penylan Road (Cwmbran)....8 F4
Penylan Road (Newport) ..16 H3
Penylan Road (Varteg) ..2 F2/G1
Penylan Way 8 G4
Penyrheol Road 4 H5
Penywain Cottages*,
Penywain Road 4 E4
Penywain Lane 4 F4
Penywain Road 4 F4
Penywain Street 4 E4
Penywain Terrace 4 E4
Penywaun Close 8 E6
Penywaun Road.......8 E5/E6/F5
Pepys Grove 19 D1
Percy Street 2 G1
Peregrine Court...............27 B5
Perry Court 7 C4
Perthy Close 8 G5
Pettingale Road 9 B4
Petunia Way 12 G1
Philanthropic Cottages 8 G2
Phillip Street (Blaenavon) ...1 B4
Phillip Street (Newport).....21 A1
Phillips Green (9) 17 A4
Phillsay House 8 G5
Phoenix Drive 32 F5
Piccadilly Lane 31 A1
Picked Lane 22 F4
Picton Road 3 A2
Picton Street 6 E2
Picton Walk......................8 E5
Picton Walk.....................20 H1
Picwic Green.....................8 E4
Piercefield Avenue 31 B2
Piercefield Cottages (2) 31 B1
Pike Cottages 25 C3

Pike Road 25 C2/C3
Pill Road 29 C1
Pill Row.........................29 C1
Pill Way.........................29 C1
Pill, The.........................29 C1
Pillmawr Circle 13 D4
Pillmawr Court*, Pilton Vale
............................13 D4
Pillmawr Road (Caerleon)..15 D1
Pillmawr Road (Newport)
............................13 D4/D5
Pilton Vale....................13 D4/D5
Pine Gardens 4 F3
Pine Grove 20 F2
Pine Tree Road..................5 D4
Pinewood Close 13 D4
Pinnell Place 19 C5
Piper Close 16 F3
Pisgah Close.....................2 H1
Pisgah Hill........................2 H1
Pisgah Road......................2 H1
Place de Cormeilles 31 C3
Plane Tree Close 15 D2
Plantation Drive 9 C4
Plantation, The 27 C4
Plas Bryn Gomer................9 A3
Plas Cwrt 10 G3
Plas Derwen 9 C4
Plas Ebbw.......................9 C2
Plas Geler Cottages*,
Green Way 2 H1
Plas Graig........................9 C2
Plas Islwyn.......................9 C1
Plas Mawr......................30 G5
Plas Trosant 9 C2
Plas Twyn 9 C2
Plas Ty Coch 10 G2
Plasycoed Road 4 F1
Playford Crescent 23 C2
Pleasant Court 3 B3
Pleasant View (5) (Pontypool)
............................3 D3
Pleasant View (Talywain) ...3 A2
Plough Road 5 B5
Plover Close 21 D6
Plover Crescent 28 G6
Plum Tree Lane 28 G4
Plym Walk......................13 D1
Pollard Close 15 D1
Pont Faen Road 21 C5
Pont y Felin Avenue 6 E3
Pont y Felin Lane 6 F4
Pont y Felin Road 6 E3
Pontaphywell.....................4 F5
Ponthir Road 15 A3
Pontnewydd Walk..............9 C2
Pontrhydyrun House 9 A3
Pontrhydyrun Road.............9 A2
Pontycraig Cottages 12 E1
Pontymason Close 12 G2
Pontymason Court 12 G2
Pontymason Lane 12 E1
Pontymason Row 12 G2
Pontymoel Turnpike 5 C2
Pontypool Bypass West 4 E4

Pontypool Road.................30 F4
Pool Lane 16 G1
Poplar Avenue 5 D4
Poplar Close 28 G2
Poplar Court 15 C2
Poplar Road (Cwmbran)....9 C3
Poplar Road (Newport) ...21 A4
Poplar Terrace (7)..............3 D3
Poplars, The 31 B4
Poppy Place 12 G1
Port Road 19 D4
Porthmawr Road................9 C1
Porthmawr Road Bungalows
............................9 C2
Porthycarne Close.............30 F5
Porthycarne Gate 30 F4
Porthycarne Street 30 F5
Portland Street 19 C6
Portman Buildings*,
Commercial Street.....4 F5
Portskewett Street............21 B2
Portwall Road 31 C4
Post Gwynne 30 H2
Post Office Row 29 D4
Post Office Terrace 15 B6
Postern (20) 8 F5
Potter Street 19 C6
Potters Croft 32 G6
Pottery Road 19 D6
Pottery Terrace 19 D5
Pound Hill 18 F1
Pound Lane 26 G2
Powells Place 33 C5
Power Street....................14 G4
Powis Almshouses*, Bridge St.
............................31 B4
Powis Close 20 H6
Prescoch Lane 4 H6/5 D1
Presteigne Walk 8 F5
Preston Avenue 19 B2
Preston Close 32 G5
Price Avenue 3 C5
Price Close (Newport).......19 C5
Price Close (Pontypool) 3 D5
Priestley Close 19 D2
Primrose Cottages 4 F3
Primrose Court 8 F3
Primrose Way 12 G1
Prince Street (Blaenavon)....1 C4
Prince Street (Newport) 33 A6
Prince Street (Pontypool)....4 F4
Princes Walk.....................5 D5
Priory Close (Caerleon) ...15 D1
Priory Close (Caldicot) 28 F5
Priory Close (Chepstow)...31 B2
Priory Court (Magor)........27 C4
Priory Court (Usk)............30 G5
Priory Crescent 23 A3
Priory Drive 23 A3
Priory Gardens 23 A3
Priory Gardens (Usk) 30 G5
Priory Grove*, Priory Way..23 A3
Priory Street 30 G5
Priory Way 23 A3
Priory, The 31 C4

Probert Place 21 A1
Proposed M4 Relief Road
............18 H1/20 H3/22 F2
Prospect Cottages 31 A5
Prospect Crescent 28 G6
Prospect Place (Abersychan)
............................3 A2
Prospect Place (Cwmbran)10 E1
Prospect Place (Pontnewynydd)
............................3 D2
Prospect Place (Pontypool) 6 E4
Prospect Place (Varteg) 2 E1
Prospect Street................14 G4
Prossers Houses................4 F3
Pugsley Street 14 H5
Pump Street 33 B3
Purcell Square 21 A5
Pwll Pen Court*,
Hartridge Farm Road..23 D1
Pwllmeyric Close.............32 E1
Pye Corner 17 C5

Q

Quantock Drive 16 H5
Quarry Cottages (Pontypool)
............................4 E6
Quarry Cottages (Undy) 27 B4
Quarry Rise.....................27 B4
Quarry Road 4 H5
Quebec Close 17 B6
Queen Street (Blaenavon) ..1 B4
Queen Street (Griffithstown)
............................6 E2
Queen Street (Newport) ...33 D4
Queen Street (Pontypool) ...4 F4
Queen Victoria Almshouses*,
Stow Hill 19 B3
Queens Close 14 H4
Queens Croft 14 H4
Queens Gardens..............27 B3
Queens Hill 33 A3
Queens Hill Crescent 33 A2
Queens Road 32 E3
Queens Way (Llanwern) ...21 D6
Queensway (Newport) 33 B3
Queensway Meadows..21 C4/D6
Quilter Close 21 B6

R

Race Road 4 G4
Rachel Square 20 G2
Radnor Road 16 G1
Radnor Way 10 E2
Raglan Close 3 A2
Raglan Court (Cwmbran) 9 A2
Raglan Court (Newport) ...19 C5
Raglan House*, Allt yr Yn View
............................14 H2
Raglan Mews 20 H1
Raglan Way.....................32 F2
Railway Cottages (Abersychan)
............................3 A3
Railway Cottages (Pontypool)
............................6 G3
Railway Street (Caerleon)..15 D4

Railway Street (Newport) ..33 A4
Railway Terrace (Blaenavon)
......................................1 C3
Railway Terrace (Caerleon)
......................................15 D4
Railway Terrace (Pontypool)
......................................6 G2
Railway Terrace (Rogiet) ..28 H1
Railway View 28 G6
Ramp Cottages................27 C5
Ramp, The 27 C5
Ramsey Walk (Cwmbran)....7 B5
Ramsey Walk (Newport)....16 G2
Rankine Close 13 D2
Rannock House 8 E5
Raphael Close 16 G2
Ravenscourt 7 D4
Rector Road 25 B4
Rectory Gardens..............27 C6
Red Hill...........................30 G6
Red House Road...............26 F5
Red Lion Flats*, Foundry Road
......................................3 B2
Redbrook House*,
    Redbrook Way 9 D2
Redbrook Road................19 A1
Redbrook Way 9 D2
Redd Landes....................26 F5
Reddings, The...................32 F4
Rede Road 8 F5
Redland Street 14 G4
Redlands, The..................21 B5
Redmeadow Crescent 28 G6
Redvers Street 21 B2
Redwick Court...................10 E2
Redwick House*, Redwick Court
......................................10 E2
Redwick Road...................27 C3
Redwood Close (Caerleon)
......................................15 D1
Redwood Close (Chepstow)
......................................32 F3
Reen Cottages*, Somerton Road
......................................21 B3
Reene Court 21 B3
Rees Close 13 C3
Regent Way 31 C3
Reginald Terrace (10).......17 A4
Rembrandt Way 16 F2
Renoir Road 16 G3
Reservoir Close 17 A5
Restway Wall 31 C4
Reynolds Close 16 F2
Rhiw Melin 7 A5
Rhodri Place (9) 10 E4
Rhuddlan Close 17 B2
Rhyd Tre Derwen 3 D2
Rhyd y Nos Street...............1 B4
Rhymney Court...................7 C4
Ribble Square...................13 D1
Ribble Walk......................13 D1
Richmond Close 9 B1
Richmond Place 9 B1
Richmond Road (Cwmbran)
......................................9 B1

Richmond Road (Newport)
......................................16 G1
Richmond Road (Pontypool)
......................................6 G2
Richmond Street 9 B1
Ridgeway (Newport) 19 B1
Ridgeway (Pontypool) 3 D6
Ridgeway Avenue.............19 A1
Ridgeway Close 19 A2
Ridgeway Court 19 A2
Ridgeway Crescent...........19 A1
Ridgeway Drive................19 A2
Ridgeway Grove 19 A1
Ridgeway Hill 19 A2
Ridgeway Park Road 19 A2
Rifle Green 1 A4
Rifle Street 1 A4
Riflemans Way 31 C3
Ringland Centre 23 C1
Ringland Circle
......................16 H6/21 A6/23 C1
Ringland Way 21 B6/23 D1
Ringwood Avenue.............16 H5
Ringwood Hill 16 H5
Ringwood Place 16 H6
Risca Road (Newport) 33 C1
Risca Road (Rogerstone) ..12 F1
Rise, The............................7 B6
Rising Sun Gardens 15 C3
River Row (17) 3 D3
River View (Chepstow) 31 C4
River View (Newport) 16 F1
Rivermead Way 12 G1
Riverside (Caerleon).........15 B3
Riverside (Garndiffaith).......2 H2
Riverside (Newport) 14 H6
Riverside (Pontypool) 4 E5
Riverside Cottages*, School La.
......................................3 A3
Riverside Court 4 F5
Riverside Drive 1 C4
Riverside Estate 15 A2/B6
Riverside Mill....................31 B5
Riverside*, The Back 31 B4
Riversmead......................10 E3
Riverview*, The Moorings ..16 F2
Roath Court 9 D3
Robbins Lane 33 C5
Robert Place 19 C5
Roberts Close..................12 G3
Robertson Way.................13 C3
Rochdale Terrace (1) 3 D3
Rochester Road 21 A2
Rock Cottages 28 E4
Rock Lodge......................25 D2
Rock Villa Close 2 F1
Rock Villa Lane 31 B5
Rockfield Close 24 F6
Rockfield Crescent 27 B6
Rockfield Glade.................24 F6
Rockfield Grove 27 B6
Rockfield House 4 E5
Rockfield Rise 27 B5
Rockfield Street 14 G6
Rockfield Way 27 B6

Rockhill Road..............4 G6/5 C1
Rockwood Cottages 31 D4
Rockwood Road 31 D3
Roding Close 12 E6
Rodney Parade.................33 A5
Rodney Road 33 A5
Rogiet Road 28 G2
Rogiet Terrace 28 G1
Roland Villas*, Freeholdland Rd.
......................................3 C3
Rolls Close 8 E4
Rolls Walk........................12 H4
Roman Gates 15 D4
Roman Reach...................15 D1
Roman Way 15 C2/C3
Romney Close 16 G3
Romsley Court 8 E6
Ronald Road.....................16 G1
Rosamund Close 20 H2
Rosary, The 4 E6
Rose Cottages (Chepstow)
......................................32 G1
Rose Cottages (Garndiffaith)
......................................2 H2
Rose Cottages (Talywain) ..2 H1
Rose Cottages (Upper Race)
......................................4 H4
Rose Cottages (Varteg) 2 E3
Rose Court 8 E3
Rose Garden, The (Newport)
......................................33 A1
Rose Gardens (Cwmbran) ..9 C4
Rose Street 33 A3
Rose Terrace (6)..................3 D2
Rose Villas*, Manor Road....3 A2
Rose Walk 12 G1
Rosebery Street 6 E2
Rosecroft Drive 23 A4
Rosemary Cottages 3 D3
Rosemary Lane...................4 F5
Rosemead 7 D3
Rosendale Court...............16 H2
Ross House*, Victoria St. ..10 E1
Ross Lane 14 G4
Ross Street 14 F4
Rosser Street 4 E4
Rosslyn Road 21 A2
Rother Close.....................11 D6
Rothesay Road 21 A2
Rougemont Grove 32 G5
Round Stables 3 B1
Roundwood Close 25 C1
Routes View 23 C4
Row, The (3) (St. Arvans)..31 B1
Row, The (Shirenewton) 26 F5
Rowan Close.....................27 B5
Rowan Court 8 F4
Rowan Crescent 6 F1/G2
Rowan Drive 32 F3
Rowan Way 13 C4
Rowland Villas 3 C3
Royal Oak Drive ...16 G6/23 B1
Royal Oak Green 9 C4
Royal Oak Hill 16 F6
Royce Walk......................12 H4

Royston Crescent 21 B4
Rubens Close 16 G2
Rudry Street 14 H6
Ruffetts Close 31 C2
Rugby Road 33 A6
Rumney Walk (10) 10 E4
Ruperra Close...................17 C4
Ruperra Lane 33 D5
Ruperra Street 33 D5
Rupert Brooke Drive 19 C2
Rush Wall 27 D2
Rushbrook 7 D4
Ruskin Avenue 12 G3/G4
Ruskin Close 8 E4
Ruskin Rise......................19 D1
Russell Close (Newport) ...17 B3
Russell Close (Pontypool) ..5 D5
Russell Drive....................13 D3
Russell Drive Gardens 13 D3
Russell House*, Richmond St.
......................................9 B1
Russell Street 9 B1
Russet Close.....................23 A4
Ruth Road...........................5 C3
Rutherford Hill...................13 D3
Rutland Place 33 D4

S

Saffron Court......................8 F3
Salisbury Close.................14 G5
Salisbury Court 7 D6
Salisbury Terrace 2 E2
Samsons Avenue 2 F2
Sandpiper Way 20 G1
Sandy Lane (Caerwent) 26 H3
Sandy Lane (Caldicot) 28 E4
Sandy Lane (Castleton) 30 F1
Sandy Lane (Newport) 20 E2
Sandybrook Close...............8 F6
Sawtells Terrace (7) 3 D2
Saxon Place 31 D6
Saxons Houses...................3 A2
Scarborough Road 16 F1
Scard Street 33 B3
School Close 4 G4
School Cottages (Mathern)
......................................32 G1
School Cottages*, Tump Lane
......................................27 C5
School Court (Cwmbran) ...10 E1
School Court (Llanvair-Discoed)
......................................25 A6
School Crescent 6 G2
School Hill.........................31 C4
School Houses*, Bailey Street
......................................19 A4
School Lane (Abersychan) ..3 A3
School Lane (Garndiffaith) ..2 G2
School Lane (Newport) 33 B4
School Lane (Pontypool).....4 E4
School Park.......................27 B4
School Road (Abersychan)..3 B2
School Road (Cwmbran).....7 A5
School Road (Penperlleni) ..5 B6
School Road (Pontypool) ...3 D3

School Road (Shirenewton) ...26 E5
School Terrace (12) (Pontnewynydd) ...3 D2
School Terrace (Rogerstone) ...17 A2
School View ...4 G6/5 C1
Scott Close ...19 D1
Scott Walk ...12 G4
Sea Street Lane ...27 D1
Sea View ...29 D3
Sea View Terrace ...28 H1
Seasons Close ...27 B3
Seaview Terrace ...19 B4
Second Street ...22 E3
Sedbury Lane ...31 B5/B6/C6
Sedgemoor Court ...14 G3
Selby Close ...10 E4
Serpentine Road ...33 A3
Seven Stiles Avenue ...21 C6
Severn Avenue ...31 B5
Severn Bridge Park Homes ...32 F6
Severn Bridge, The (M48) 32 H5
Severn Crescent ...31 D4
Severn Terrace ...33 C3
Severn View (Caldicot) ...28 G4
Severn View (Chepstow) ...31 C3
Severn View (Cwmbran) ...7 A4
Severn View (Garndiffaith) ..2 G2
Severn View Terrace ...3 B2
Sevins (21) ...8 F5
Seymour Avenue ...24 E6
Seymour Rise ...24 E6
Shaftesbury Court (4) ...14 H4
Shaftesbury Street (5)...14 H5
Shaftesbury Walk (6) ...14 H5
Shakespeare Close ...28 G3
Shakespeare Crescent ...19 C1/D1
Shakespeare Drive ...28 G3
Shakespeare Road ...8 E6
Shakespeare Row*, Shakespeare Drive ...28 G3
Shannon Close ...13 D2
Sharps Way (3) ...32 F5
Shaw Grove ...19 D1
Shawley Court...8 E6
Shea Gardens*, Francis Drive ...19 C5
Sheaf Lane ...33 A6
Shelley Close ...28 F3
Shelley Green ...8 E6
Shelley Road...21 A2
Shepherd Drive...24 H2
Shepherds Hill Caravan Site ...4 H4
Sherbourne Court...6 G2
Sherbourne Road ...6 G2
Sheridan Close ...19 D1
Shetland Close ...16 G2
Shetland Walk ...16 G2
Shires, The ...30 G2
Shop Road ...2 E2
Shop Row ...27 D1

Shops, The*, The Uplands 12 H5
Short Path (22) ...8 F5
Shrewsbury Close (7) ...14 H5
Sickert Close ...16 G3
Sid Griffiths Court ...2 H2
Sidney Street ...33 B2
Silleys Close ...31 A5
Silver Birch Close ...15 D1
Silver Fir Square ...17 B5
Simpson Close ...13 C3
Sims Square ...21 A5
Sir Charles Crescent ...20 G2
Sir Charles Square ...20 G2
Sirhowy Court ...7 C4
Siskin Crescent*, Barn Owl Rd. ...28 G1
Sixth Street ...22 F4
Skenfrith House ...13 A3
Skenfrith Mews ...20 H1
Skinner Lane*, Skinner Street ...33 B4
Skinner Row ...21 B5
Skinner Street ...33 B4
Slade Street ...21 B2
Slade View ...28 G1
Slate Houses ...3 D2
Slate Row ...2 E2
Slipway Cottages ...22 F2
Sluvad Lane ...6 E6
Sluvad Road ...6 E5
Smallbrook Close ...10 E2
Smithfield Cottages ...18 G4
Snail Creep ...2 E2
Snail Creep Terrace ...2 E3
Snatchwood Court ...3 C3
Snatchwood Road ...3 C3
Snatchwood Terrace...3 B2
Sneyd Park*, Malpas Rd. ..13 C3
Snowdon Court ...9 B3
Soane Close ...12 G4
Soar Close ...9 B4
Soho Street ...21 A1/A2
Somerset Cottages ...31 B4
Somerset Road (Cwmbran) ...9 C2
Somerset Road (Newport) ...16 G1
Somerset Way...32 F4
Somerton Cottages*, Cromwell Road ...21 B2
Somerton Court ...21 C3
Somerton Crescent...21 A4
Somerton Lane ...21 B3
Somerton Park ...21 B3
Somerton Place*, Chepstow Rd. ...21 A4
Somerton Road ...21 A3/B3
Sorrel Drive ...33 A2
South Avenue ...6 G1
South Close ...10 F4
South Court (16) ...3 D3
South Grove ...28 G1
South Lake Drive ...18 G6/H6
South Market Street ...33 D5

South Road...10 G2
South Row ...27 D1
South Street ...6 G2
South View (Chepstow) 31 B5
South View (Llanvaches) ..25 B3
South View (Pontnewynydd)3 C3
South View (Pontypool)...4 F4
South View Terrace (8)...1 C4
South Walk ...9 D1
Southbrook View...29 C2
Southern Distributor Road 18 H4
Southville Road...33 B1
Sovereign Arcade*, Kingsway ...19 B5
Spartan Close ...23 A4
Speke Street ...21 A1
Spencer Road...33 C2
Spinney, The...13 D4
Spouts Hill ...26 F6
Spring Gardens...19 C5
Spring Grove ...7 D3
Spring Lane ...9 C3
Spring Street ...14 F4
Spring Terrace ...6 F1
Springfield Close (Cwmbran) ...9 A3
Springfield Close (Newport) ...17 B1
Springfield Court ...23 D5
Springfield Drive ...16 H6
Springfield Houses (8) ...3 D2
Springfield Lane ...17 B1
Springfield Road (Newport)17 B1
Springfield Road (Pontypool) ...6 G1
Springfield Terrace (Pontnewynydd) ...4 E1
Springfield Terrace (New Inn) ...6 E4
Springfield Villas*, Wainfelin Rd. ...4 E4
Springfields ...30 F2
Springvale ...7 C5/D5
Springvale Way...7 C6
Spytty Lane ...21 C3
Spytty Road...21 C3/C5
Square, The (Abersychan) ..3 B3
Square, The (Cwmbran) ...7 A3
Square, The (Magor) ...27 C3
Squires Close ...12 H4
Squires Gate...12 H4
Squirrel Cottages ...31 B1
St. Andrews Avenue ...31 D4
St. Andrews Close ...9 A2
St. Ann Street ...31 B4
St. Annes Close (Cwmbran) ...9 C1
St. Annes Close (Newport) ...17 A5
St. Annes Crescent (Newport) ...16 G1
St. Annes Crescent (Undy)27 C6
St. Anthonys Close ...6 F1
St. Arvans Court ...31 B1
St. Arvans Road ...9 D2

St. Augustine Road ...6 F1
St. Basils Crescent ...17 C4
St. Basils Stores ...17 C4
St. Benedict Close...6 F1
St. Benedict Court...17 C4
St. Briavels House*, Oaksford ...8 E3
St. Briavels Mews ...20 H1
St. Brides Close (Cwmbran) ...10 E4
St. Brides Close (Magor)....27 B3
St. Brides Crescent ...20 E2
St. Brides Gardens ...20 E2
St. Brides Road...27 A3
St. Cadocs Close ...15 C3
St. Cadocs Road...3 D6
St. Cecilia Court*, Gold Tops ...19 A4
St. Cybi Avenue ...24 F1
St. Cybi Drive ...24 F1
St. Cybi Rise ...24 F1
St. Davids Close (Chepstow) ...31 D4
St. Davids Close (Pontypool) ...4 E6
St. Davids Court (Magor) ..27 C3
St. Davids Court (Marshfield) ...30 H3
St. Davids Crescent ...19 D2
St. Davids Road ...9 C2
St. Dials Court*, St. Dials Road ...7 D6
St. Dials Road ...7 D5/D6
St. Dominics Retreat...4 G4
St. Donats Close (11) ...10 E4
St. Dubricius Gardens...27 C6
St. Edward Street ...33 C3
St. Ewens Road ...32 E4
St. George Road...31 D4
St. Georges Crescent...16 G2
St. Georges Way...32 F6
St. Hildas Road ...6 F2
St. James Field ...4 F5
St. Johns Close...4 E3
St. Johns Court (Rogerstone) ...12 H2
St. Johns Court*, Oakfield Road ...19 A3
St. Johns Crescent (Pontypool) ...4 E3
St. Johns Crescent (Rogerstone) ...12 H2
St. Johns Gardens ...31 C2
St. Johns Road ...16 H2
St. Joseph Place...10 H4
St. Josephs Close...27 C6
St. Julians Avenue ...16 G1
St. Julians Court ...16 G1
St. Julians Lodge*, Haisbro Av. ...16 F1
St. Julians Park*, Stockton Road ...14 F6
St. Julians Road ...16 G1
St. Julians Street...33 C3
St. Kingsmark Avenue ...31 B2

St. Lawrence Lane 31 D1
St. Lawrence Parc........31 C1/C2
St. Lawrence Road 31 B2
St. Lukes Close..................3 A2
St. Lukes Road 3 D3
St. Marks Crescent 33 A2
St. Martins Court...............19 C2
St. Mary Court.................33 B3
St. Mary Street (Chepstow)
.................................31 C4
St. Mary Street (Newport) .33 C3
St. Marys Close..................6 E1
St. Marys Crescent 28 G1
St. Marys Place.................29 C2
St. Marys Road (Cwmbran) 9 C3
St. Marys Road (Nash) 22 H5
St. Marys Street (Pontypool)
....6 E1
St. Marys Way 30 G5
St. Matthews Road......4 G6/5 C1
St. Maur Gardens 31 B3
St. Maur House*, St. Maur Gdns.
.................................31 B3
St. Mellons Close 27 B5
St. Mellons Road 30 H2
St. Michael Grove 10 H4
St. Michael Street 19 C6
St. Michaels Court 19 C6
St. Michaels Mews 19 C6
St. Oswalds Close 6 G2
St. Peters Close 8 E4
St. Peters Close*, Ty Gwyn Rd.
.................................8 F4
St. Phillips Flats*, Cromwell Rd.
.................................21 B2
St. Stephens Close...........26 G3
St. Stephens Court 27 C6
St. Stephens Place 27 B6
St. Stephens Road 19 D6
St. Tathans Place 26 G3
St. Tecla Road 32 E3
St. Teilo Road..................27 C6
St. Tewdric Road 31 D3
St. Tewdrics Place 32 G1
St. Thomas Court 3 A1
St. Vincent Court*,
Corporation Road 33 A5
St. Vincent Lane 33 A5
St. Vincent Road 33 A5
St. Woolos Court...............33 C3
St. Woolos Green 9 C2
St. Woolos Place 33 C3
St. Woolos Road...............33 C3
Stable Row 1 B3
Stafford Road (Caldicot)...28 G5
Stafford Road (Newport)...14 G6
Stafford Road (Pontypool) .5 D1
Stamford Court 14 H4
Stanford Road...................21 A6
Stanley Place 9 C1
Stanley Road (Garndiffaith) 2 G2
Stanley Road (Newport) 33 A3
Star Lane 3 D5
Star Road 5 B6
Star Street........................10 E1

Star Villas 15 A3
Starling Close*, Barn Owl Road
.................................28 G1
Station Approach (Caerleon)
.................................15 D4
Station Approach (Newport)
.................................17 C4
Station Bungalows 29 B4
Station Close*, Station Road
.................................28 G4
Station Cottages 10 F4
Station Farm 9 C3
Station Houses 2 E3
Station Road (Caerleon) ...15 D4
Station Road (Caldicot)......28 H4
Station Road (Chepstow) ..31 C4
Station Road (Cwmbran) 9 B1
Station Road (Llanwern) ...23 D3
Station Road (Ponthir)..15 A1/B5
Station Road (Pontypool) 6 E2
Station Road (Portskewett)
.................................29 B4
Station Road (Rogiet)........28 G1
Station Street (Abersychan) 3 B3
Station Street (Newport) ...33 B3
Station Terrace (Blaenavon)
.....................................1 C4
Station Terrace (Cwmbran)..9 B1
Station Villas 15 A1/B5
Steep Street 31 C3
Steepfield 9 B3
Steer Crescent 16 G3
Stelvio Park Avenue 33 D1
Stelvio Park Close.............19 B2
Stelvio Park Court.............33 D1
Stelvio Park Crescent 33 D1
Stelvio Park Drive 33 D1
Stelvio Park Grove 19 B2
Stelvio Park Rise 33 D1
Stelvio Park View 19 B2
Stephen Walk*, Cefn Wood
.................................17 A4
Stephenson Street ..19 D6/22 E1
Stepping Stones 5 A5
Sterndale Bennett Road ...23 C1
Stevelee 8 F5
Stevenson Close...............12 H4
Stevenson Court 12 H4
Steynton Path 8 E5
Stiels...............................8 G5
Stockton Close 16 E1
Stockton Road...................14 F6
Stockwood Close*, Silure Way
.................................23 A4
Stockwood View 23 A4
Stokes Cottages*, Stokes Drive
.................................15 B6
Stokes Court 15 A2/B6
Stokes Drive 15 A2/B6
Stone Cottages.................29 D4
Stoney Road......................2 H2
Stour Court 7 C4
Stow Hill 33 C2/C4
Stow Park Avenue 33 C2
Stow Park Circle 33 D1

Stow Park Court*, Stow Hill
.................................19 B4
Stow Park Crescent 33 C1
Stow Park Drive 33 D2
Stow Park Gardens...........33 D1
Stowe Path (12) 10 E4
Straits Lane.....................22 H6
Strand, The 9 D1
Striguil Road 32 E3
Strongbow Road...............31 D4
Stuart Avenue 31 B2
Sudbrook Road.................29 C3
Sudbury Walk 14 G5
Sullivan Circle 21 A6
Summerhill Avenue 16 H1
Summerhill Court (7) 2 G1
Summerhouse Lane 32 F5
Sunbeam Close 21 B1
Sunlea Crescent 5 B3
Sunningdale Court 16 H5
Sunny Bank (Blaenavon) 1 A3
Sunny Bank (Garndiffaith) ..2 H2
Sunny Place 15 A5
Sunnybank (Cwmbran)........8 G2
Sunnybank (Newport).......17 C2
Sunnybank Court 6 E2
Sunnybank Road 6 E1
Sunnybank Way 6 F1
Sunnyside (Penperllleni) 5 A6
Sunnyside (Usk) 30 F6
Surrey Place....................16 G1
Sussex Close 21 C3
Sutherland Crescent........16 G3
Sutton Road 14 G6
Swallow Drive..................28 G5
Swallow Way 20 F1
Swan Close 28 G5
Swan Square 3 A2
Sward Close 12 G4
Swinburne Close...............16 H3
Sycamore Avenue (Caldicot)
.................................28 F4
Sycamore Avenue (Chepstow)
.................................32 F3
Sycamore Avenue (Newport)
.................................21 A3
Sycamore Court (Chepstow)
.................................31 B1
Sycamore Court (Cwmbran)
...................................8 G2
Sycamore Place 7 B5
Sycamore Road 6 F1
Sycamore Road South 6 G1
Sycamore Terrace 27 C4
Sycamores, The*, Albion Road
.....................................4 G4
Sychan Terrace..................3 B2
Sylvan Close....................13 C4
Symondscliffe Way 29 C1

T

Tabernacle Road 25 B3
Taff Court 7 B4
Taff Road.....................28 E5/F5
Talbot Lane......................33 C4

Talfan Close 3 C5
Talgarth Close...................10 E2
Taliesin 9 C1
Taliesin Close 12 H4
Taliesin Drive 12 H4
Tallards Place 31 C6
Tallis Close 23 D1
Talywain House*, Woodlands
....2 H1
Tamar Close 14 E2
Tan House Court 26 G3
Tan House Drive 16 E5
Tan y Coed 3 D3
Tatton Road 22 E6
Teal Close........................27 B5
Tees Close 13 D2
Tegfan Court......................8 G3
Telford Close 12 H4
Telford Street 21 A1
Tempest Drive 31 C2
Tempest Way 31 C2
Temple Street 19 C6
Tenby Close (Cwmbran).......9 D4
Tenby Close (Newport).....20 H1
Tenison Road 3 D6
Tennyson Avenue*, Station Rd.
.................................23 D3
Tennyson Close 28 G3
Tennyson Road (Newport)
.................................21 A2
Tennyson Road (Caldicot)
.................................28 G3
Tern Court.........................7 C4
Terrace, The 29 C3
Terry Morgan Bungalows 1 C5
Tetbury Close 14 G5
Tewdrick Court 9 C4
Tewends (23) 8 F5
Tewkesbury Walk (8) 14 H5
Teynes 8 F5
Thames Close...................14 E1
Third Street 22 E3
Thirlmere Place 16 F1
Thistle Court 8 E3
Thomas Grove 17 A4
Thomas Street 31 C3
Thompson Avenue 21 B4
Thompson Close...............21 B4
Thorn Tree Drive (5) 32 F1
Thornbury Park 17 A4/B4
Thornbury Park Shop. Centre*,
Thornbury Park.........17 A4
Thorncliffe Court 8 E5
Thornhill Centre 7 C4
Thornhill Close 7 A4
Thornhill Gardens.............12 G2
Thornhill Road 7 C5
Thornhill Way 12 G2
Thornwell Road 32 E4/F4
Till Grove 15 C1
Tillsland 8 G5
Tintern Close....................10 E2
Tippet Close 23 C1
Tirpentwys Terrace 4 E2
Tolpath 8 F3

Tom Mann Close 16 G6
Ton Bach Street 1 C4
Ton Mawr Avenue...............1 C4
Ton Mawr Road 1 C4
Ton Mawr Street..................1 C4
Ton Road (Cwmbran) 8 E4/F5
Ton Road (Llangybi) 24 F1
Ton Road Cottages............24 F1
Tone Close 11 D6
Tone Road 11 D6
Tone Square.....................11 D6
Top Road 2 G2
Torfaen Terrace (19)............3 D3
Toronto Close 17 B6
Torridge Road...................11 D6
Tower Court*, London St...16 H1
Towers, The 9 D2
Town Bridge Buildings*,
   Pontaphowell.................4 F5
Tram Cottages 10 H5
Tram Lane 10 H6
Tram Road (Caerleon) 15 D4
Tram Road (Cwmbran) 7 A4
Tramway Close 8 F3
Tranch Road 4 F3
Trannon Court......................7 C4
Tranquil Place 10 F1
Tranters Terrace 7 A5
Traston Avenue 21 D4
Traston Close 21 D4
Traston Lane.....................21 D4
Traston Road 22 E2
Traws Mawr Cottages........13 B1
Traws Mawr Lane 13 C1
Treberth Estate........16 H6/23 B1
Tredegar Court 19 D5
Tredegar Drive 27 B5
Tredegar House Drive 20 G1
Tredegar Park View 17 B5
Tredegar Street (Newport)
   ....19 B6
Tredegar Street (Rhiwderin)
   ....17 B1
Trees Close 13 D2
Treetops 29 B2
Tregare Street...................33 D5
Tregarn Close...................24 G2
Tregarn Court 24 G2
Tregarn Road 24 H1
Tregwilym Close 17 B4
Tregwilym Road 17 A2/A4/B3
Tregwilym Walk.................17 B4
Treherbert Road 9 A4
Trelawney House*, Mary Street
   ....30 G5
Trelawny Close 30 F6
Trellech Close...................10 E2
Trem Twyn Barlwm 10 F1
Trem y Mynydd Court 1 C5
Trent Road 11 D6
Tretower Court (13)...........10 E4
Trevine Path 8 E5
Trevithick Close 13 C2
Trinity Court 19 C6
Trinity Lane.......................15 D2

Trinity Place 19 C6
Trinity Road 7 C6/9 B1
Trinity View 15 D1
Troddi Close 28 E5
Trosmawr Road*, St. Dials Rd.
   ....10 E1
Trosnant Street.............4 G5/G6
Trosnant Villa 4 G6
Trostrey 8 G5
Trostrey Close 5 D5
Trostrey Street 14 H6
Trostry Lane 25 A4
Trussel Road 9 C2
Tubular Cottages 31 B5
Tudor Court.......................27 C5
Tudor Crescent 17 A4/A5
Tudor Drive.......................31 C2
Tudor Road (Cwmbran) 9 D1
Tudor Road (Newport) 16 F1
Tudor Woods 10 E4
Tulip Walk 12 H1
Tump Lane 27 C5
Tunnel Terrace 33 C2
Turberville Road 9 C2
Turner Street.....................14 H6
Turners End (26)................8 F4
Turnpike Close (Chepstow)
   ....31 C2
Turnpike Close (Pontypool)
   ....5 C3
Turnpike End.....................32 F6
Turnpike Road 9 C4/10 E4
Turnstiles, The 14 G5
Tutshill Gardens 31 B5
Tweedy Lane 21 A2
Twin Cottages 15 A3/B6
Twinings, The 8 E4
Twisells Road 4 F3
Twm Barlwm View 10 E4
Twmbarlwm Rise.................8 F2
Twmpath Gardens 4 G4
Twmpath Road 4 F4
Two Locks Road 8 F6/10 F1
Twyn Court*, Twyn Sq.....30 G5
Twyn Oaks 15 C5
Twyn Square 30 G5
Ty Box Close.......................9 B1
Ty Box Cottages 9 C1
Ty Box Road........................9 C1
Ty Brith Gardens 30 G5
Ty Canol Court 8 F3
Ty Canol Row 8 F3
Ty Canol Way 8 E2
Ty Coch Close 17 C3
Ty Coch Lane
   ....10 G1/H2/13 A2/A3
Ty Coch Terrace*, Ty Coch La.
   ....10 G1
Ty Coch Way.....................10 F1
Ty Coed 7 B4
Ty Draw 6 G6
Ty Draw Lane 6 G6
Ty Dwmpyn Road 4 E1
Ty Fry 1 B4
Ty Fry Close 1 B4

Ty Graig Home*, Pillmawr Road
   ....13 D4
Ty Gwyn Road (Cwmbran)
   ....7 D5/8 E3
Ty Gwyn Road (Little Mill) ..6 G6
Ty Gwyn Road (Varteg) 2 F2
Ty Gwyn Way 7 D4
Ty Helyg*, Willow Close 21 C4
Ty Mawr Lane...................30 H3
Ty Mynydd 9 C2
Ty Mynydd Close 1 B5
Ty Palmyra*, Palmyra Pl. ..33 C4
Ty Pwca Place 7 A5
Ty Pwca Road.....................7 A5
Ty Rosser Gwyn 2 G2
Ty Trappa Place 7 B6
Ty Trappa Road 7 B6
Ty Tudor 9 D2
Tydies.................................8 G5
Tydu View 17 A5
Tylers Way 31 C6
Tyllwyd Road 33 B1
Tyn y Nant Cottages..........18 H1
Tyne Close 12 E6
Tynewydd Avenue 9 B1
Tynewydd Court 9 B1
Tynewydd Drive 30 F1
Tynewydd Farm Close 9 A1
Tynewydd Green.................9 B1
Tynewydd House*,
   Tynewydd Road 9 B2
Tynewydd North Close 9 A1
Tynewydd Road 9 B2
Tynewydd South Close.......9 B1

Ullswater Court 7 D5
Underwood Shopping Centre
   ....7 D5/8 E3......23 D6
Union Street 3 B2
Upland Drive.......................3 C4
Uplands Court (Newport) ..16 H2
Uplands Court (Rogerstone)
   ....12 H3
Uplands Terrace 7 D6
Uplands, The 12 H3
Upper Brick Yard 1 A3
Upper Bridge Street 4 F5
Upper Church Street.........31 C4
Upper Coed Cae 1 B5
Upper Cwmbran Road 7 A4
Upper Dock Street 33 B4
Upper Five Houses 2 E1
Upper Garn Terrace 1 A2
Upper Glantorvaen Terrace 1 C3
Upper Hill Street 1 B4
Upper Nelson Street 31 C4
Upper Park Terrace.............4 F5
Upper Power Street 14 G4
Upper Tennyson Road 16 H2
Upper Trosnant Street 4 G5
Upper Waun Street 1 B3
Upper Woodland Street 1 B4
Upton Lane 33 C1
Upton Road........................19 B2

Usk Bridge Mews 30 G4
Usk Close 28 E5
Usk Court 7 D4
Usk House (Cwmbran) 10 H2
Usk House*, Allt yr Yn View
   ....14 H2
Usk River Crossing............21 C1
Usk Road (Caerleon) 15 D4
Usk Road (Penperlleni)........5 B6
Usk Road (Pontypool)
   ....5 A4/B3/C3
Usk Road (Shirenewton)...26 E5
Usk Street.........................14 G6
Usk Vale Close 15 D4
Usk Vale Drive 15 D4
Usk Vale Mews 15 D4
Usk Vale View...................16 E5
Usk View 16 F3
Usk Way ..19 D5/20 E5/33 B5/D6
Uskside 15 D3
Uskside Cottages*, Uskside
   ....16 E5
Uskvale Court 5 B3

V

Vale View (Cwmbran) 8 G2
Vale View (Newport)..........16 G3
Valentine Lane 32 F5
Valentine Road 3 B3
Van Dyke Close 16 G2
Vanbrugh Close 12 H4
Vanbrugh Gardens 19 D2
Vancouver Drive......17 B6/19 B1
Varteg Road 1 C4/2 F1
Varteg Waste 2 F1
Varteg Waste Road.............2 F1
Vaughan Williams Drive 21 A5
Vauxhall Lane...................31 C3
Vauxhall Road 31 D3
Ventnor Road 10 E2
Vermeer Crescent 16 G3
Vernon Grove 26 H3
Veronica Close 17 B5
Viaduct Court 4 G6/5 C1
Viaduct Road 2 H2
Viaduct View*, Ambleside Upper
   ....2 H1
Viaduct View*, Viaduct Rd...2 H2
Vicarage Close 17 C4
Vicarage Court 30 G2
Vicarage Gardens (Caerwent)
   ....26 G3
Vicarage Gardens (Marshfield)
   ....30 G2
Vicarage Gardens (Newport)
   ....12 G2
Vicarage Hill 33 C4
Vicarage Lane.....................2 H3
Vicarage Terrace 2 H3
Vicars Cottages*,
   Maesderwen Road 5 C1
Victoria Avenue.................16 H1
Victoria Close 33 C4
Victoria Court 16 H1
Victoria Crescent..............33 B3

Victoria Lane....................**16** H2
Victoria Mews*, Victoria Place
..............................**33** C4
Victoria Place (Abersychan) **2** H2
Victoria Place (Newport)....**33** C4
Victoria Place*, Viaduct Road
..............................**2** H2
Victoria Road (Abersychan) **2** H2
Victoria Road (Chepstow) ..**32** F4
Victoria Road (Newport) **33** C4
Victoria Road (Pontypool)
..............................**4** G6/5 C1
Victoria Street (Cwmbran)..**10** E1
Victoria Street (Pontypool) ..**6** E2
Victoria Villas (10)...............**3** D3
Victoria Walk*, Commercial St.
..............................**19** A5
Victoria Way **27** B5
Villas, The **29** C4
Vincent Street **1** B4
Vine Cottages (3) (Caerleon)
..............................**15** D4
Vine Cottages (Chepstow) **31** D3
Vine Place..........................**16** H1
Vinegar Hill **27** A5
Violet Walk **12** G1
Viscount Evan Drive **20** F2
Vivian Road.......................**21** A1

W

Wades, The (25) **8** F5
Waghausel Close **28** G5
Wainfelin Avenue **4** E4
Wainfelin Road **4** E4
Walden Grange Close.......**21** A4
Walford Davies Drive **21** A5
Walford Street...................**14** G4
Walk Farm Drive **30** E1
Walk, The **5** D4
Walkdens, The (27)............**8** F5
Walker Flats **29** D4
Wallace Close **30** F6
Wallis Street **19** C6
Walmer Road **21** A2
Walnut Drive **15** D1
Walsall Street **21** B1
Walton Close.....................**21** B5
Waltwood Park Drive **23** C6
Waltwood Road **23** D5
Ward Close........................**16** G3
Warlock Close...................**23** C1
Warren Slade **32** F4
Warrendale (28) **8** F4
Warwick Close (Chepstow)
..............................**32** E3
Warwick Close (Cwmbran) ..**7** D3
Warwick Close (Pontypool)..**6** F4
Warwick Lane*, Warwick Road
..............................**21** A3
Warwick Road...................**21** A3
Watchhouse Parade **19** D5
Waterloo Cottages **10** F1
Waterloo Court **6** G2
Waterloo Place **3** A2
Waterloo Road (Newport) ..**19** C4

Waterloo Road (Talywain) ..**3** A2
Waters Lane **33** B4
Waters Road.....................**31** D4
Waterside Close **12** G3
Waterside Court (Newport) **14** F5
Waterside Court*, Abbey Road
..............................**10** E1
Waterside Walk West **12** H3
Waterworks Lane **2** H3
Watkins Walk*, Cefn Wood
..............................**17** A4
Watt Close (Newport) **13** C3
Watts Close (Rogerstone) **12** H5
Waun Allt y Rhyd **3** D1
Waun Blis **9** A3
Waun Cottages.................**10** G6
Waun Hywel Road **7** B6
Waun Road **8** F6
Waun Wern..........................**4** G3
Waun Wern Caravan Park ..**4** G3
Waunddu **3** D2
Wavell Drive **13** C3
Waveney Close.................**11** D5
Waverley Terrace.......**4** G6/5 C1
Wayfield Crescent..............**9** C1
Weare Close.....................**11** D6
Webley Close **15** B3
Webley Gardens **15** B3
Wedgwood Drive **29** C3
Wednesbury Street...........**21** B2
Weldon Close **9** B4
Well Close (6) **32** F5
Well Cottages (Magor) **27** C1
Well Cottages (Portskewett)
..............................**29** B3
Well Lane **25** A6
Welland Circle...................**11** D5
Welland Crescent **11** D5
Wellfield Court **30** H2
Wellfield Lane **6** G2
Wellfield Road...................**30** H2
Wellington Drive **7** D4
Wellington Lane **4** F3
Wellington Road (Newport)
..............................**17** B6
Wellington Road (Talywain)
..............................**3** A1
Wells Close **19** D2
Wellwood Cottages (11) **3** D3
Welsh Street **31** B2
Wentloog Close **9** D2
Wentsland Crescent **4** F3
Wentsland House*,
Wentsland Road **4** G3
Wentsland Road................**4** G3
Wentwood Close.................**7** B5
Wentwood Drive (Llanvaches)
..............................**25** B3/B4
Wentwood Drive (Parc-Seymour)
..............................**24** E6
Wentwood Road **15** D1
Wentwood View **28** E5
Wentworth Close...............**17** B2
Wern Fach Court **8** G3
Wern Hill **4** F4

Wern Road **6** G2
Wern School Close.............**6** G2
Wern Terrace (Newport) **12** H3
Wern Terrace (Pontypool)....**4** F4
Wesley Close **10** E1
Wesley Place **33** B4
Wesley Street **10** E1
Wesley Terrace...................**4** E1
West Avenue **6** G1
West Bank.........................**10** E4
West Bank Court (25) **3** D4
West End (Magor)..............**27** C3
West End (Undy) **27** C5
West End Avenue................**3** C3
West End Cottages (Caldicot)
..............................**27** C5
West End Cottages (Magor)
..............................**27** C3
West End Gardens **27** C5
West Hill Road **3** C4
West Market Street............**33** D5
West Nash Road................**22** H6
West Park Road **19** B2
West Place **4** F5
West Roedin **8** G5
West Street **33** B3
West View **7** D6
West View Terrace **1** B2
West Way Road **20** E5
Western Avenue (Chepstow)
..............................**32** F4
Western Avenue (Newport)
..............................**17** B6
Western Valley Road **17** B5
Westfield **28** F4
Westfield Avenue (Caldicot)
..............................**28** F4
Westfield Avenue (Newport)
..............................**13** D4
Westfield Close **15** C2
Westfield Drive **13** D3
Westfield Road (Caerleon) **15** C2
Westfield Road (Newport)..**33** B1
Westfield Way....................**13** D3
Westgate Court.................**15** D4
Westmoor Close **21** C5
Weston Villas **29** B4
Westray Close **16** G2
Westville Road **19** A2
Westway **28** G1
Weyloed Lane **26** E5
Wharf Lane **21** A1
Wharf Road.......................**21** A1
Wheatsheaf Court.............**27** C4
Wheeler Street **14** G5
Whistler Close...................**16** F2
Whitby Mews*, Whitby Pl...**14** H6
Whitby Place.....................**33** A6
White Ash Glade...............**15** D2
White Avenue **20** H1
White Hart Lane **16** E4
White House Gardens **6** H6
White Houses......................**3** D1
Whitebrook Way **10** E2
Whitechapel Walk **27** B5

Whitegate House **3** D3
Whitehall Gardens **27** C5
Whitehall Lane **10** E4
Whitehouse Close...............**9** C4
Whitehouse Road **9** C4
Whitet Houses.....................**3** B1
Whitethorn Way **30** H3
Whitewall **27** C4
Whitstone Road **16** H4
Whittakers Row..................**7** A4
Whittle Court **13** C3
Whittle Drive **13** C3
Wiesental Close **28** F5
Wilcrick Place **9** B2
Will Paynter Walk*,
Kier Hardie Drive........**16** G6
Willenhall Street **21** B1
William Brown Close.........**10** H3
William Lovett Gardens....**33** B2
William Morris Drive **16** G6
William Street **9** C1
Williams Close*, Francis Drive
..............................**19** C5
Willins **8** F5
Willow Close (Caldicot) **28** F4
Willow Close (Chepstow) ..**32** E3
Willow Close (Newport) **21** C4
Willow Close (Rogerstone) **12** G1
Willow Drive **23** D5
Willow Green **15** C2
Willows, The (Cwmbran).....**9** C3
Willows, The (Redwick) **27** D1
Willows, The (Undy) **27** C4
Wills Row (12)....................**17** A4
Wilson Road **16** G3
Wilson Street **19** C6
Wimbourne Rise **7** C5
Winchester Close **19** D3
Windermere Court **7** D5
Windermere Square **16** F1
Windmill Cottages **28** F1
Windmill Farm Lane **25** B4
Windmill Lane...................**28** G1
Windmill Square **33** D5
Windrush Close.................**14** E1
Windsor Close **27** C3
Windsor Drive **27** C3
Windsor Gardens **27** C3
Windsor Park **27** C3
Windsor Place (13) **17** A4
Windsor Road (Cwmbran) ..**8** E5
Windsor Road (Newport) ..**21** A2
Windsor Road (Pontypool)..**6** E2
Windsor Terrace **33** B3
Wingate Street **19** D5
Winmill Street **33** D6
Winstone House **2** H3
Winstone Road **3** D4
Wintour Close **31** B2
Wirewood Close **31** A5
Wirewood Crescent..........**31** A5
Wisteria Close...................**13** C4
Wiston Path........................**8** F5
Witham Street **21** A1
Withy Close.......................**27** C4

Withy Walk 27 C4
Withyrea Cottages..............14 F3
Wolseley Close..................19 D6
Wolseley Street..................19 D5
Wood Close (Cwmbran) 10 F4
Wood Close (Newport) 12 G3
Wood Crescent..................12 G3
Wood House 4 E5
Wood Path 9 B3
Wood View*, Coed Cae Place
....4 G4
Woodbine Cottages (Pontypool)
....4 F1
Woodbine Cottages (Usk)..30 F6
Woodbine Gardens.............27 C4
Woodfield Road 5 D4
Woodland Court 9 C3
Woodland Drive (Bassaleg)17 C3
Woodland Drive (Rogerstone)
....12 F1
Woodland Park Road 16 H2
Woodland Road (Cwmbran) 9 C3
Woodland Road (Newport) 16 H2
Woodland Road (Underwood)
....23 D5
Woodland Street (Blaenavon)
....1 B4
Woodland Street (Cwmbran)
....7 D6
Woodland Terrace (9)
(Pontypool) 3 D2
Woodland Terrace (Varteg) 2 E3
Woodland View (Caldicot)..28 F4
Woodland View (Garndiffaith)
....2 F1
Woodland View (Pontypool) 4 E4
Woodland View (Rogiet)....28 G2
Woodlands (Talywain) 2 H1
Woodlands Close 31 A1
Woodlands Drive 13 C3
Woodlands Estate..............13 C4
Woodlands Roundabout 13 B3
Woodlands, The (Pontypool)
....4 E6/5 A1
Woodlands, The *,
Waterworks Lane 2 H3
Woodley Houses...................1 C6
Woodpecker Close*,
Barn Owl Road..........28 G1
Woods, The 3 D2
Woodside (Newport) 20 F1
Woodside Road (Cwmbran) 9 C1
Woodside Road (Pontypool)
....3 C4
Woodside Terrace 9 C1
Woodside Villas 3 C3
Woodside Way 7 C5
Woodside*, Berthon Road ..6 H5
Woodstock Close 28 G4
Woodstock Court 28 G4
Woodstock Way 28 G4
Woodview Court 4 G4
Woodview Terrace*, Albion Rd.
....4 G4
Woodville Road..................19 A2

Woolpitch 7 D4
Woolpitch Wood 31 D1
Worcester Close 9 D3
Worcester Crescent 16 F2
Worcester Path 9 D3
Wordsworth Close (Caldicot)
....28 G4
Wordsworth Close (Cwmbran)
....8 E6
Wordsworth Road 21 A2
Wrenford Court*, Commercial St.
....33 B4
Wright Close 21 C3
Wye Court 7 D4
Wye Crescent (Chepstow) 31 D4
Wye Crescent (Newport) ..13 D1
Wye Valley Link Road........32 E2
Wye View Houses*,
Buttington Road 31 D5
Wyebank Avenue 31 C5
Wyebank Close...................31 C5
Wyebank Crescent 31 C5
Wyebank Drive 31 C5
Wyebank Place...................31 C5
Wyebank Rise.....................31 C5
Wyebank Road 31 C5
Wyebank View 31 C5
Wyebank Way.....................31 D5
Wyecliffe*, Castleford Hill ..31 B4
Wyelands View..................32 G1
Wyeverne Road 21 A3
Wyndcliffe Court 31 A1
Wyndcliffe Houses*,
Buttington Road 31 D5
Wyndcliffe View..................31 B1
Wyndham Street................14 H5
Wyngate Street..................19 D5
Wyntour Houses*, Buttington Rd.
....31 C6

Y

Yellow Row...........................4 G3
Yeo Close 14 E1
Yetts, The 31 D6
Yew Tree Close (Caldicot) 28 G4
Yew Tree Close (Undy) 27 C5
Yew Tree Flats 10 G1
Yew Tree Lane 15 D4
Yew Tree Rise 28 G2
Yew Tree Terrace
(Croesyceiliog) 9 B3
Yew Tree Terrace (Cwmbran)
....10 E1
Yew Tree Wood 31 C1
Yewberry Close 13 D4
Yewberry Lane 14 E4
Yewtree Cottages 6 E5
Ynys Lane 9 B3
York Close 7 D4
York Place 33 C2
York Road...........................16 G1
Ysgol Place.........................7 A5

Z

Zion Hill*, Pentrepoid Rd. 3 D3

HOSPITALS
Blaenavon Hospital..............1 B3
Chepstow Community Hospital
....31 C2
Gwent County General Hospital
....5 D1
Llanfrechfa Grange Hospital
....10 E5
Royal Gwent Hospital 33 D4
St. Anne's Hospice 13 C4
St. Cadoc's Hospital 15 D3
St. David's Foundation 16 H2
St. Joseph's Hospital 13 C4
St. Woolos Hospital 33 D3

POLICE STATIONS
Alway Police Station 21 A5
Bettws Police Station 13 D1
Blaenavon Police Station 1 C3
Caerleon Police Station ...15 D4
Caldicot Police Station 28 F5
Castleton Police Station 30 E1
Chepstow Police Station....31 C3
Cwmbran Police Station 9 D2
Cwmbran Police Divisional HQ
....9 D4
Duffryn Police Station 20 F1
Fairwater Police Station 8 F4
Garndiffaith Police Station ..2 G2
Llanover Police Station 1 A5
Magor Police Station..........27 C4
Maindee Police Station......16 H1
New Inn Police Station 6 E4
Newport Police Divisional HQ
....33 D5
Pill Police Station 19 D6
Pontypool Police Station 4 F5
Rogerstone Police Station 17 A4
Trevethin Police Station 3 D5
Underwood Police Station 23 D6
Usk Police Station 30 G5

SCHOOLS & COLLEGES
Abersychan School.............3 A3
Alway Infants & Junior School
....21 A5
Archbishop Rowan Williams CW
Prim. School 29 B3
Bassaleg School................17 C4
Bettws High School............14 E2
Brookfield Primary School..10 E1
Brynglas Primary School....14 E4
Caerleon Comp. School 16 E3
Caerleon Endowed Inf. & Jun.
Schools 16 E4
Caerleon Lodge Hill Inf. & Jun.
Schools 15 C2
Caldicot Comp. School......28 G5
Chepstow Comp. School ..31 B2
Clytha Primary School 33 C1
Coed Eva Inf. & Jun. Schools
....8 F4
Coleg Gwent
(Pontypool Campus) 4 G4
Coleg Gwent
(Newport Campus) 21 D5
Crindau Primary School 14 G5
Croesyceiliog Inf. & Jun. Sch. ...
....9 B3
Croesyceiliog School 9 D4
Crownbridge Special Sch....6 F2
Cwmffrwdoer Prim. School ..3 D2
Dell Primary School 31 C3
Duffryn High School 20 G3
Duffryn Inf. & Jun. Schs. 20 F2
Durand Prim. School 28 G5
Durham Road Infants Sch. 14 G6
Durham Road Junior Sch. 14 G6
Eveswell Primary School ..21 A2
Fairwater High School.........8 E4
Fairwater Inf. & Jun. Schools
....8 E5
Gaer Infants School 19 C2
Gaer Junior School............19 C2
Garnteg Primary School.....2 G2
George Street Prim. Sch.....4 E4
Glasllwch Primary School ..19 B1
Goytre Fawr Prim. School....5 B5
Green Lane Jun. Sch. 28 F4
Green Lawn Junior School ..5 D4
Greenmeadow Prim. Sch....7 D3
Griffithstown Infant & Nursery
School 6 E2
Griffithstown Junior School ..6 F2
Hartridge High School........23 D1
Henllys CW Prim. School 8 F3
High Cross Prim. School....17 A5
Hillside Primary School.......1 B4
Hollybush Primary School....8 F5
Kemys Fawr Infant School ..6 G1
Kimberley Nursery School..14 F3
Langstone Prim. School 24 G1
Liswerry High School 21 D5
Liswerry Inf. & Jun. Schs. ..21 C4

Llanmartin Prim. School ...23 D5
Llantarnam School 10 H3
Llanyrafon Prim. School 10 E3
Maendy Primary School.....9 C1
Maes Ebbw School 20 E3
Maesglas Primary School ..20 E3
Magor Inf. & Jun. Sch. 27 C4
Maindee Primary School....33 B6
Malpas Court Prim. Sch.....13 C3
Malpas CW Inf. & Jun. Schools
...................................14 E4
Malpas Park Prim. School 13 C4
Marshfield Inf. & Jun. Schools
...................................30 F1
Mathern Nursery School....32 G1
Millbrook Inf. & Jun. Schools
...................................13 D2
Milton Inf. & Jun. Schools ..23 B2
Monnow Inf. and Jun. Schools
...................................12 E6
Mount Pleasant Prim. School
...................................12 G4
New Inn Infant School.........5 D4
Oakfield Primary School....10 G3
Offa's Mead Prim. School..31 C5
Osborne Nursery School ..16 H5
Our Lady of the Angels
RC Prim. School 10 E1
Pembroke Inf. & Jun. School
...................................32 F4
Pentrepoeth Prim. School..17 C2
Pentwyn Primary School......3 B2
Penygarn Inf. & Jun. Schs ..3 D6
Pillgwenlly Prim. School ...19 C5
Ponthir Primary School 15 A5
Pontnewydd Prim. School....7 B6
Pontnewynydd Prim. Sch...3 C3
Pontymoile Prim. School 4 G6
Portskewett Inf. Sch...........29 C3
Ringland Inf. & Jun. Schs...21 A6
Risca Comp. School 12 E1
Rogerstone Prim. School ..17 A4
Rogiet Primary School 28 G1
Rougemont Lower School..19 A1
Rougemont School 13 B3
Sandy Lane Inf. Sch. 28 E4
Shirenewton Prim. Sch. 26 E5
Somerton Primary School..21 A4
St. Alban's RC High Sch. 4 F5
St. Alban's RC Prim. Sch. 4 F4
St. Andrew's Inf. & Jun. Schools
...................................21 B2
St. David Lewis RC Prim. Sch.
...................................13 D2
St. David's RC Primary School
(Newport)...................20 E2
St. David's RC Primary School
(Cwmbran)...................9 B2
St. Francis RC Farm. Sch. 3 A2
St. Gabriel's RC Prim. School
...................................16 H6
St. John's-on-the-Hill Sch. 31 B4
St. Joseph's RC Prim. School
...................................16 H1
St. Josephs High School ..20 G1

St. Julian's High School 16 F2
St. Julian's Inf. & Jun. Schools
...................................16 G3
St. Mary's Jun. School
(Caldicot) 28 F5
St. Mary's RC Inf. & Jun. Sch.
(Chepstow) 31 D3
St. Mary's RC Prim. School
(Newport)...................33 A3
St. Michael's RC Prim. School
...................................19 D5
St. Patrick's RC Prim. School
...................................21 B3
St. Peter's CW Prim. Sch.....1 B3
St. Woolos Prim. School 33 C3
Thornwell Inf. & Jun. Schools
...................................32 F5
Trevethin Community School
...................................4 E5
Two Locks Nursery Sch. 10 F1
Undy Primary School 27 C5
University of Wales College
(Allt-yr-yn Campus) 33 A1
University of Wales College
(Caerleon Campus) ...15 C3
Usk Primary School 30 G6
Victoria Primary School 2 H3
West End Inf. School 28 G4
West Monmouth School 4 G4
Woodlands Inf. & Jun. Sch...7 B4
Wyedean School...............31 C6
Ysgol Bryn Onnen.............2 E2
Ysgol Gyfun Gwynllyw 3 D5
Ysgol Gymraeg Casnewydd
...................................23 D1
Ysgol Gymraeg Cwmbran....8 E6
Ysgol y Ffin 29 D4

INDUSTRIAL ESTATES

ARD Business Park 5 D3
Abersychan Ind. Estate.......3 B3
Albany Trading Estate 14 G5
Avondale Industrial Estate ..9 B2
Boxer Industrial Estate 15 B3
Bulwark Industrial Estate ..32 E4
Caligo Court 7 D5
Celtic Springs Business Park
...................................18 G4
Cheesemans Ind. Estate ..28 G2
Cleppa Park 18 G4
Cleppa Park Ind. Estate 18 F5
Court Road Ind. Estate 10 F3
Crawford Trading Estate....14 G6
Crindau Industrial Estate....14 F5
Cwmbran Retail Park 9 D1
Daniel Doncaster Ind. Estate
...................................1 B2
East Retail Park 20 E4
Enterprise Park Ind. Est....19 C6
Evtol Trading Estate 19 C6
Felnex Industrial Estate 22 E2
Forge Hammer Ind. Estate ..9 D1
Frederick Street Industrial Area
...................................19 C6
Gilchrist Thomas Ind. Est....1 B2
Grange Industrial Estate ...10 E2
Gwenallt Industrial Estate 4 E1
Harlech Retail Park............19 D3
Herbert Road Ind. Area 14 G6
Heritages Court..................1 B2
Hill Street Ind. Estate 10 F1
Ifton Industrial Estate 28 F2
Ifton Quarry Ind. Estate 28 G2
Imperial Park 18 G6
Jacks Pill Ind. Estate.........33 D6
Johnsey Trading Estate 21 B1
Kay's & Kear's Ind. Estate....1 B2
Langstone Business Village
...................................23 A3
Lee Way Industrial Estate ..22 E5
Llandevenny Development Site
...................................27 C1
Llantarnam Industrial Park
...................10 G2/H2/H3
Lower Mill Industrial Estate..5 D2
Lyne Road Industrial Area..14 F5
Maesglas Industrial Estate 19 D4
Mill Lane Industrial Estate..31 C4
Mill Parade Ind. Area 19 D6
Mitel Business Park 29 B1
Mon Bank Sidings Development
Site 19 C4
Neptune Works 20 E6
Newhouse Farm Ind. Est...32 G4
Newport Docks Ind. Area ..20 F6
Newport Retail Park 21 C6
Old Town Dock Development
Site 21 C1
Oldbury Business Centre ..10 E1
Panteg Industrial Estate 6 E2

Pavilion Estate 3 D4
Pill Farm Industrial Estate..29 D1
Polo Grounds Ind. Estate 5 D3
Pontnewynydd Ind. Estate ..4 E3
Pontnewynydd Small
Business Centre 4 E2
Pontyfelin Industrial Estate ..6 E3
Pontypool North Ind. Park....4 E3
Queensway Meadows Ind. Est.
...................................21 D5
Rafiki Leisure Park 9 B2
Reevesland Ind. Estate......22 E3
School Hill Trading Estate 31 C4
Sedbury Business Park 31 C6
Severn Bridge Ind. Estate..29 C1
Skillian Business Centre 22 F7
Somerset Industrial Estate ..9 C2
South Pontypool Ind. Park ..5 D3
Springvale Industrial Estate 7 C5
Star Trading Estate............15 B3
Station Yard Ind. Estate 31 C4
Stephenson Street Ind. Estate
...................................22 E1
Torfaen Business Centre 5 D3
Traverner Trading Estate ..15 D4
Tregwilym Industrial Estate17 B4
Ty Coch Distribution Centre
...................................10 G1
Ty Coch Industrial Estate ..10 F1
Wern Industrial Estate 12 H3
Western Industrial Estate ..15 C4